TEENS

Paul Bühre was fifteen years old when he wrote this, goes to high school, and wants to be a comic-strip artist when he's grown up. He lives with his parents in Berlin.

TEENS

What we're really thinking
(when we're not saying anything)

Paul Bühre

Translated by David Shaw

SCRIBE
Melbourne • London

Scribe Publications
18–20 Edward St, Brunswick, Victoria 3056, Australia
2 John Street, London, WC1N 2ES, United Kingdom

Originally published in German as *Teenie Leaks* by Ullstein in 2015
First published in English by Scribe in 2016

Front cover image: iStock 56346948

Typeset in Minion Pro 11/16pt by the publishers
Printed and bound in the UK by CPI Group (UK) Ltd, Croydon CR0 4YY

CIP records for this title are available from the National Library of Australia and
the British Library

9781925321036 (Australian edition)
9781925228342 (UK edition)
9781925307375 (e-book)

scribepublications.com.au
scribepublications.co.uk

Contents

Preface xi

1   **Group Dynamics** 1
or, what's really going on when a horde
of apparently happy teenagers rampage through
the corridors of their school

2   **Social Networks** 21
or, what's in our heads when we're staring at our
phones instead of out in the fresh air playing football

3   **Looks** 33
or, why boys don't show off their underpants
in public anymore

4   **Drugs and Alcohol** 47
or, what people are like when their parents smoked
weed and they grew up watching a TV show where
a chemistry teacher runs a meth lab

5   **Computer Games**   61
     or, why gamers don't go on killing sprees

6   **Sex and Porn**   81
     or, why there's still room for just holding hands

7   **School**   97
     or, why it would be better if some teachers were
     a bit more like the meth-cooking chemistry teacher
     from Chapter 4

8   **The Blue Skeletons of November**   109
     or, what we're listening to when we're wearing
     our headphones

9   **Conflict with Parents**   123
     or, why you should never call your kids any
     stupid nicknames

10 **Parenting** 139
or, what you need to know according
to a person directly affected by the issue

11 **Mood Swings** 151
or, what to take seriously (while not freaking out)

12 **Me and Others** 161
or, what teens care about besides themselves

Acknowledgements 173

Preface

So how did I, a fifteen-year-old teenager, end up writing a book about teenagers? It all started with a school internship at *Zeitmagazin* in Berlin. This lasted three weeks, and I met a lot of very cool and nice people there.

At the beginning of the internship, I had a lot to do — proofreading articles mostly. But after I'd finished my work, I started to get bored and so they gave me a new exercise: write about your everyday school life. So I wrote around twenty pages. I didn't think anything of it at the time; it was just fun being occupied with work. Then I met Heike, a really cool journalist who really helped me to structure my article. She also showed it to the editor-in-chief of *Zeitmagazin*, who decided to print my piece as the title story of the next issue.

I was really surprised and very happy, because I would never have imagined that I would be able to write and publish an article in a great magazine like *Zeit*. After the article was published, Heike showed it to her literary agent, who then called and asked me if we could meet. That's how I met

Alexander Simon — and he asked me if I would like to write a book. 'Chances like this don't happen every day,' I thought, so I said yes.

We found a publisher for me, and I started writing 500 words every day, which I then sent to Heike, who guided me the entire time. After half a year of work, the book was done.

1

Group Dynamics

or, what's really going on when
a horde of apparently happy
teenagers rampage through
the corridors of their school

Nothing — and I mean really nothing — is as confusing as the many different social groups in my school. Most adults, when they think of their children's school, imagine a group of happy boys and girls frolicking through the corridors or playing football out in the playground. But that's just a tiny part of what goes on behind those walls. Every day is a battle for social standing and respect. Pretty much like *Game of Thrones*. Only with WhatsApp and hundred-metre races instead of swords and dragons.

I can identify three broad groups among the thirty-or-so kids in my class. Anything more intricate than that is beyond me, but these groups are in fact further divided into sub-groups and sub-sub-groups.

So, first there's Group A. This is the coolest-sickest-awesomest-gangsta-school's-a-pile-of-shit group, which everybody wants to be in, and which I, to my own astonishment, am a member of. This group's school's-shit attitude kicked in about three years ago. Before that — so, into the first year of high school — some of us still

3

tried to do well in tests, paid attention in class, sucked up to teachers, and did our homework, or at least took the time to copy it from someone else. The rest already saw teachers as the embodiment of all-that-is-evil, yet did their schoolwork, albeit grudgingly. All that was long ago. Now we're all on the same page: the cool kids with bad grades, who hate teachers and school in general, who think their parents are just cringe-worthy, who love to spend money, especially on brand labels, who like sports and gaming (but aren't hardcore gamers, they're in a different group), the TV junkies, film junkies, Facebook-video junkies, Facebook-video-likers, misogynist joke-tellers, posers, expensive-smartphone-owners, those who know a lot about music, or think they do, the party people, pubescent people, the mega-mature, the ones who've started using deodorant … How I ended up in this group is a story I'll come back to later.

But first, to Group B. You can imagine the kind of person who's in this group: basically, anyone who can't get into Group A. This includes those who still haven't hit puberty, the wusses, and the geeks. Really, I have nothing against geeks; I like geeks. I'm one myself, just not the physics-type geek. More a kind of superhero-comic-*Star-Wars-Lord-of-the-Rings-Harry-Potter-Game-of-Thrones* book nut. That's book *nut*, not book*worm*. It's a very important distinction, because the two words describe individuals with completely different reading habits. A bookworm is someone who will spend years slowly, doggedly, laboriously slogging their way, week by week, to the end of a book, and who would shrivel up and die if their supply of reading matter ever ran out. A nut, on the other hand, can go for months without books, only to devour just as many as the bookworm, but in a matter of days. A binge like that will leave you with no appetite for reading for at least a month or so.

In any case, the geeks from Group B, the real ones, are useful for explaining some of the trickier aspects of maths, biology, physics, chemistry, or (classical) music. In return, I might sketch them something for their art project, or explain to them how to do the long jump properly (for those who are interested: take off from one leg, not two). Group B has a lot more members than Group A, since the entry requirements are not as strict. But even within Group A there's an outer and an inner circle.

Group B is also the one for those who still burst into tears when they get a bad grade — either out of fear of their parents' reaction or due to some kind of disappointment. So, for them, schoolwork is still really important, although that puts them in an extreme minority. I mean, we're in Year Ten; what do you expect? They're the ones who still run out into the playground as soon as the bell rings, cheering 'Foootbaaall!' excitedly as they go. Showing a spirit of enthusiasm rarely seen among members of Group A. And if it does arise, it usually gets nipped in the bud pretty quickly.

And then there's the third group, Group X47MKKD-89SY. As the name implies, this group is extremely complex, and rather different from the others. It's made up of all the female members of my class. If you're wondering why I lump them all together, the answer is simple. with girls, everything is in a constant state of flux. Friendships can be forged one day, and by the next morning they're gossiping behind each other's back or bitching openly. No one can trust anyone, except their best friend, but she's … you know what I mean. It's a tangled web of lies, conspiracies, secrets, dramas, tears, angst, anger, and a good portion of action — a real thriller, in fact.

But, of course, girls also come in different types: there's the gum-chewers, who always seem to look both stressed and bored at the same time; the screamers whenever an insect comes anywhere near; the constant gigglers; the ones who wear make-up (majority); the ones who don't (minority). Then there are those who refuse to do sport because it might ruin their hairdo or make them break out in a disgusting sweat, and who spend every break preening themselves; those who talk non-stop and get told off in every lesson; the shy ones; the sensitive ones … There's every type of girl in our class, but, as far as I can see, they never really form real, fixed groups — just like molecules of gas.

The fifteen-minute break is a good time to observe the different behaviours of each group. In a lesson like physics, maths, or chemistry, there will often be an argument between members of Group B. About the formula for photosynthesis or the finite nature of infinity, for example. Stuff normal people aren't really interested in. When the lesson is over, the argument carries on into the break. It usually ends with a decision to call in the teacher as umpire, to say who is right and who is wrong. The winner then gloats loudly, 'Hah! I told you so, Tom!' That might even draw in a couple of curious spectators, almost exclusively members of Group B, needless to say.

The most emotional arguments are those that pit boy against girl. Usually, all the boys side with the boy, and all the girls with the girl. Typical arguments are: Is horseriding a sport? Why be vegan when barbecues are so brilliant? Which bands or singers are cool and which are not? This is one of those rare occasions when Group A and Group B are allies, because now they have a common enemy. The boys start cracking dumb jokes to provoke the girls, who reply with a sarcastic 'Ha ha, very funny!' and a serious, grown-up look on their face. Girls always take situations like this far too seriously, anyway, and they tend to bear a grudge. But, unfortunately, arguments like this only happen rarely.

Normally what happens is that Group A and some of Group B don't argue, but do everything they can to try to stay indoors, copy their homework from someone, play games, or watch videos on their phones, and to generally shelter from the weather.

Anyway, Group A only ever leave the classroom if they're told to do so by a strict teacher. The only other reason to leave is to buy vital provisions in the cafeteria.

Group Member 1: 'Hey, let's go to the cafeteria. It's dead boring here.'

Group Member 2: 'Yeah, let's go.'

And so the whole group can end up spending the entire break standing in the queue, only to realise that nobody wanted to buy anything anyway. Sometimes we do go outside, but not for long:

1: 'Let's go outside.'

2: 'Cool.'

1: 'Let's go back in.'

2: 'Cool.'

While this is going on, Group B have usually been out playing football in the playground, and come back in red-faced and panting. We're more into energy conservation. Anyway, just hanging and doing nothing is usually cooler than actually doing something. School is hard enough work as it is.

And what are the girls doing while this is going on? They're out in the playground, sitting in a circle, on their phones. The whole break long. The size of the circle of girls might vary, but this is their normal behaviour. And when I say 'on their phones', I'm not talking about playing games; they're texting. Talking and texting — these are their two favourite pastimes. Girls never play games. Not even *Temple Run* or *Doodle Jump* and harmless stuff like that. Nothing. I think they think playing games is immature. They prefer to be all grown-up, and then go home and watch the mega-mature and totally thrilling *High School Musical* movies, starring Zac Efron.

Now to the question of how I ended up in Group A, and what business I have being in it at all. I need to rewind a bit here. When I started at my combined primary and secondary school in Year Five, I played quite a bit of rugby, or at least I tried to. In the first three years, it was pretty cool. A sport like that bonds you together as a team. Victories and defeats, injuries, trips to play in tournaments … And part of Group A is made up of rugby players, so the rest is history. Anyone who doesn't play rugby but wants to get into Group A just needs to act as if he couldn't care less about what group he's in. And not over-try to be funny or anything.

So that more or less explains how I ended up in Group A. Thinking about how to describe my role within the group, I read through an article I found online about 'group dynamics', and actually recognised myself in it. First, there is a leader (Alpha), and that's definitely not me. Then there's the group's opponent, or victim, known as 'G', and that's not me either. I'm also not Beta (Alpha's adviser) or Gamma (simple group member, follower). I am Omega. Omega has the most text in the article, so must be the coolest. In the interest of explaining my vital role, here's a little exchange between members of Group A:

Alpha: 'Hey, G, what's up with your hair?'

G: 'Huh? What do you mean? Is there something wrong with it?'

Alpha: 'You've got something in your hair, just here!' (Gives G's ear an unceremonious flick. The aim is to aggravate the victim, and usually provokes a feud of tit-for-tat ear-flicking. A flick to the ear might look innocuous, but it actually really hurts.)

All Gammas: 'Ha ha, fucked in the ear! Cool, Alpha.'

Omega looks on as the scene unfolds. He utters not a word, but inside he's seething.

Beta, Alpha's number one arse-licker, suddenly appears as if from nowhere, grabs G's pencil case, and brandishes it like a trophy.

Omega's every muscle is now taut. But still he does not intervene.

G: 'Aww, man, Beta, give me my pencil case back!!'

Beta (to the Gammas): 'Did you hear that, guys? He wants his pencil case back!!!' (His eyes flash.)

Before Omega's inner eye, Beta, who he's always seen as quite a nice guy, metamorphoses into a monster. With a terrifying gesture, Beta raises his hand and points at G, who in turn looks imploringly at Alpha. But Alpha now seems bored by the whole thing, and looks straight through the victim, as if he wasn't even there.

Now it is time for Omega to step in. This means me!

Omega's emotion levels have crossed a critical point. He strides resolutely towards Beta. He would dearly love to punch him, but knows he can't, because Beta hasn't done anything to him directly — and because Beta is actually just a pathetic, insecure little boy, and Omega even feels slightly sorry for him. Omega draws a deep breath and, with an almost disinterested voice, addresses Alpha: 'Can you guys stop messing round and just give him his pencil case back?'

Alpha is now rocking nonchalantly on his chair: 'I haven't got it. Tell Beta.'

With a sigh of irritation, Omega turns to Beta: 'Can you give him his pencil case back now?'

Beta: 'Aww, man, Omega, it's just a bit of fun.'

Omega glares at Beta, until the latter shrugs his shoulders, rolls his eyes, and throws G his pencil case.

All Gammas: 'Aww, Omega, why do you have to take everything so seriously?'

Yeah, I'm really sorry for being such a killjoy, but if you're ever in a situation like that yourself, you'd like someone to come to your rescue, too. Not a word of gratitude from G. Not that Omega expected any thanks, but he's a bit disappointed nonetheless. Especially the next day, when Beta and G swap roles, with G now gleefully taunting Beta. Somehow, everybody has to take a turn being the victim, and nobody seems to realise that they could just as easily be the one getting teased. The roles can flip faster than you think.

Of course, there are a couple of people who are perpetual victims. It might be because they're too sensitive to provocation, or because they're crap at football, or maybe their school grades are too good and they like to show off about how they didn't even do any work and still got an 'A'. Or they might just be too shy to fight back.

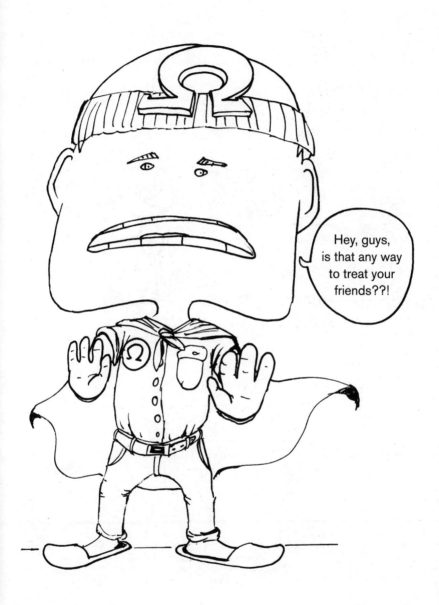

HAPPY ENDING

Manoeuvring yourself out of a situation like that is not easy. It's not usual to get parents or teachers involved, and certainly not the conflict mediators that some schools bring in. Those morons usually just make things worse, and the two adversaries end up hating each other even more.

There's a lot of talk at school about bullying and cyberbullying, and they're always making us sign bits of paper promising not to break the rules. But, to me, those signed commitments are just a bit of an escape clause for school and students alike. Bullying? What bullying? No, there's no bullying here! The proof is in black and white on the walls of the office entrance hall; everybody signed it.

Yet if bullying should still raise its ugly head, despite the signed commitments to the contrary, the best thing is to give certain people — those who have a need to feel superior to others — a wide berth and to react to them as little as possible. But what you have to remember is that not everyone is like that. So if someone unexpectedly says 'Hello' to you, and maybe doesn't mean it as a taunt, then 'Yeah, very funny' or 'Leave me alone' are not the right ways to respond.

However, if someone comes up to you and is clearly looking for trouble, then just take them aside, tell them openly how they're making you feel, and just ask them to leave you in peace. It's a tightrope walk, but if you push everyone away because you're scared of getting hurt, you'll just end up lonely and alone.

2

Social Networks

or, what's in our heads when
we're staring at our phones
instead of out in the fresh air
playing football

They've been around for quite a while now: a species of teenager that should really be adults' favourite. A species that doesn't make a lot of noise or puke on the footpath at six in the morning. On each individual, two round objects cover his ears. Two leads connect those objects to a smartphone, on which a choice of the latest games is being played (of course, the popularity of apps changes constantly, and different apps are more or less popular with different sub-groups even at my school). The subject's face is a mask of concentration, aggression, or boredom, depending on whether he has just set a new record, has just missed a new high score, or is simply very bored. In general, if you have nothing else to do, you can always check your phone. My friend Bartholomew, for example (name changed; he's a really serious case) — it's impossible to have a conversation with him for more than about three minutes without him beeping, ringing, or flashing, and replying to some message or other on WhatsApp. It's a pain in the arse.

Even during break times at school, people play football

less than they did at primary school because they're all tapping and swiping their phones, engrossed in a game, or busy sending pictures on Snapchat. The idea behind Snapchat is simple: you take a photo, send it to your friends, they get to look at it for maybe five seconds, and it automatically deletes itself. The aim is to get a picture of someone looking as goofy as possible; then you can write a witty comment or draw a little picture of a penis on it.

This brings us to the issue of some teenagers' online activity, beginning with Facebook. There is no other social network of any relevance. (Apart from Instagram, that is, for those of a more artistic bent, where you can share creatively altered pictures of your pet or your dinner. But Instagram is not that popular with the people in my class — unlike Facebook, which is used by ninety per cent of students. The remaining ten per cent are only not on Facebook because their parents won't allow it. What *that* leads to is something I'll come back to later.)

I'll start by trying to outline some of the positive aspects of Facebook. It makes arranging to meet up with friends very easy (much easier than simply calling them). Facebook helps you re-establish contact with people you haven't heard from for ages (although that might make you realise precisely *why* you haven't been in touch with them for so long). People are constantly sharing little videos on Facebook, a few of which are actually really funny — like the one with a toddler saying '*Oh, hello motherfucker!*' Others are not so funny, and some are just disgusting. Yes, disgusting, in any of a number of ways: pornographic, violent, or a mixture of both. Don't worry, those videos get taken down from Facebook pretty quickly. Apart from that, Facebook is the place you can let the whole world know you are now 'in a relationship' with someone. Another thing Facebook is good for is as a way to establish contact with the girl of your dreams, even if you don't really know her personally. Send a quick friend request along with a profile pic you've touched up a bit with a photo editor, and then casually start a conversation on Messenger:

Boy: 'Hi!'

Girl: 'Do I know you?'

B: 'You do now. You like *Twilight*?'

G: 'Edward!!!'

B: 'Yeah, right? Totally cool …'

I don't actually know any boys who really think *Twilight* is cool, because it's a show about two boys, one a vampire, the other a werewolf, fighting over a beautiful but insecure girl. The main suitor is called Edward, has perfect manners and good looks, and has supernatural strength, too, of course. He's from a rich family and is far more mature than the pubescent, pimply youths that populate our real world. A perfect object for girls to project their dreams and desires onto. So it's not very surprising that we guys don't have much time for Edward and his cronies. But talking about things that interest girls just happens to be the most efficient way of ingratiating yourself with them, and it's much easier to lie via chat than to someone's face. Also, it takes much less courage than talking to someone in person, and, in the end, it makes a better impression.

A comparable situation in the wild:

Tom happens to meet the girl he likes, along with her eight female bodyguards who she never leaves the classroom without.

Tom: 'Hi, I'm Tom.'

Bodyguard-girl 1: 'So?'

Penny, the girl of Tom's dreams: ... (Says nothing — too shy because her friends are there, or just doesn't like Tom — he probably doesn't even watch *Twilight*.)

Tom, to bodyguards: 'I wanted to talk to Penelope — alone.'

Bodyguard-girl 8: 'Well, she doesn't want to talk to you — right, Penny?'

Penny, daunted by the bodyguards: 'Right. Let's get out of here.'

Facebook is definitely the better option.

Another good thing about Facebook is that you can find out important information about the girl of your dreams. Who she's friends with, what music she listens to, what films she likes, where she's been on holiday, who likes her photos, whose photos she likes, and who might be a new rival for her affections. We call this 'stalking', but it has nothing to do with the more extreme version of stalking in the real world, when a stalker secretly follows someone's every move and takes pictures of them in secret. No, this is just a way of finding out more about a person you're interested in without her knowing, or it's just a way of checking out what she's up to.

Now we come to the negative side of Facebook. The worst thing of all is people who desperately try to friend every single person on Facebook, even people they have never met, just so that they can show off about their three hundred 'friends'. Boys pose like male models, girls pout into the camera, and then there are people who post some stupid picture of themselves smoking or hanging around at KFC and, as if that wasn't bad enough, post some philosophical quote on their profile that they have copy-and-pasted off Wikipedia. Which makes it all the more obvious that they don't have the slightest idea what it means, because they're only twelve years old. For instance: 'What is pleasant is the activity of the present, the hope of the future, the memory of the past (Aristotle)'.

In general, Facebook has a high annoyance potential, because everyone on it tries to present themself as the coolest, most interesting person ever. Some people post things just to let other people know how epic their lives are. And then there's that annoying #loveyouguys. Urggh! I'm happy you get on so well, really I am, and that you like partying, and that you found time to take a break from partying so hard and having so much fun to post about it on Facebook.

Another thing nobody needs is all the information that is of little or no relevance to those not directly involved: 'Hanging at the mall, then off to McDonald's with BFF'. Yeah, great! Good for you. Really, I couldn't give a shit. No, I'm not green with envy because you've been out shopping;

I'll just head quietly for my favourite comic shop, thank you very much. I mean, I don't post stuff like this: 'Having best kebab ever with my mates.'

Some girls seem to enjoy doing each other's make-up and then pretending to be models for the camera. That's all well and good, if only they didn't insist on posting the pics on Facebook to feed their need for likes and comments:

A: 'OH NOOOO! YOU LOOK SOOOO PRETTY!!!!'

B: 'Oh, thaaaanks'

C: 'So pretty!!'

D: 'Pretty pretty pretty!!'

E: 'You should be a model!'

That's bound to go to a person's head after a while.

Boys do everything they can to get likes, too, of course. Our problem is achieving the right balance. On the one hand, you want your post to be liked, but, unlike girls, boys can get too many likes. I mean, when a boy posts twenty-four weird photos of himself staring thoughtfully into the distance, he can be sure the other boys won't approve. Either because they're jealous or because they pounce on any opportunity to call someone 'gay'. So I do envy the girls a little bit for that.

But not everyone is obsessed with attracting as many likes as they can. There are other ways of using Facebook:

- to constantly stream to the world what you're thinking and where you are, and to share absolutely everything with the community
- to watch or post funny videos

- to play Facebook games and constantly ask people to send you gifts
- to keep posted about events, like at the abovementioned comic shop or at your sports club, which you might otherwise miss.

For my part, I'm usually engrossed in playing some Facebook game or other, so I tend to spam people with posts about my game progress. But there are worse things. Likes and comments from parents never go down well. For most people, these are a death sentence or a kind of minus-like.

Accepting a friend request from a parent — if they're even on Facebook — is mostly okay, as long as they are not active users, and don't constantly post new profile pics, for example, or even worse, leave comments on their children's pages. 'That's a lovely picture, dear! My little star! That's my favourite picture!' No. Just no!

And when parents won't let you go on Facebook?

To be honest, you're not really missing all that much. Most group chats at our school now take place on WhatsApp, and the one or two videos that make the rounds on Facebook and are worth seeing will also be on YouTube. In my class, not being on Facebook doesn't mark you as a rank outsider. But if you don't have WhatsApp either, it can be difficult to keep in contact with your friends.

WhatsApp, for those of you who have spent the last five years in a coma or who still have a keypad phone, is an app that allows you to chat with your friends. If you want to arrange to meet or can't do your homework, you use WhatsApp. Almost nobody actually makes phone calls anymore. Of course, this makes it much easier to cancel a time to meet. You just write: 'Sry man, cant make it. Gotta study.' Especially when you don't have to study.

The fact is that we aren't really capable of doing anything without the internet. If you're looking for the nearest supermarket, there's no need to ask your parents or any other human being. You just ask Siri, or google it. If you're bored, you play a game online. If you have no idea where you are, you use Google Maps.

I'm one of those people who are always leaving their phones at home by mistake, so all this doesn't apply so much to me. And I always delete the game I'm playing on my phone just when it's at its most entertaining. After twenty minutes of playing, I start asking myself what exactly it is I'm doing.

But when we went on a camping trip with school, I was pleasantly surprised: two weeks with no internet access, and no one had withdrawal symptoms. Instead of going online, we played volleyball over a washing line, kicked a football around with some other kids, and even sang songs together. Although everybody spent the entire return trip on the coach talking about all the great things they were going to do when they got back online (such as gaming or watching films, including, yes, porn), nobody really complained seriously about missing the internet during the two weeks of camping.

And adults are no better, by the way. Just because most of them are dunces when it comes to technology, they are no happier without internet access than we are — they just don't like to admit it.

3

Looks

or, why boys don't show off their
underpants in public anymore

When it comes to their looks, teenagers have more in common with fish than just the fact that they hang around in schools. In every school, each individual is an almost exact copy of all the others, or at least tries to be. Every now and again, some new 'big fish' swims up and declares himself leader of the school. The group may not even particularly like him, but follows him anyway, for whatever reason. And then there are always a couple of misfits who don't even bother trying to go with the flow, and might even turn on the group and attack it from time to time. The swarm is constantly twisting and turning and changing direction, but the golden rule is — only the most adaptable individuals survive.

The 'big fish' defines the fashion code, and the rest of the school must live by the code. There are those who blindly follow the code, others who are well aware of its existence but fight against it with all their might, yet others who simply ignore it, and still others who scorn it. Of course, there are also those who don't even realise there *is* a code.

Here's an example of how the code works in the wild. Peter is new to the school and is feeling insecure and so on. In the hope of being accepted by his classmates, he puts on all his most expensive gear: Nike Air trainers, Tommy Hilfiger socks, and, hopefully, Hugo Boss underpants, too. (There's more about underpants soon, so be patient.) He might not know the clothing codes at his new school yet, but he knows the general rule: if you wear brands, the group will accept you. Not that people who don't wear brands won't be accepted — as long as they have something akin to a personality or attractive/useful qualities like self-confidence or helpfulness towards others. Though, of course, no one can see this at first glance. That's why it's not a bad idea for a new boy or girl to wear their most expensive gear to school at first.

Then there's the (small) anti-brand faction: George is new to the school and is feeling insecure … He wants to make sure his classmates know from the start that he couldn't give a shit about brands, or that he considers comfort more important than image. But to be recognised as 'anti' by the small minority in the class who feel the same, and to be accepted as one of their group, he also has to wear the right clothes. This means wearing brands nobody's ever heard of, or brands with logos that are so small they're almost invisible. This makes him a very different creature to those who don't even have the foggiest idea that there is a code and just wear random clothes. For example, a lovely jumper chosen by their mum, or any other kind of clothing that a normal fifteen-year-old would not be seen dead wearing, let alone alive. (In Year Twelve, even an embarrassing jumper can suddenly mutate overnight from a total no-no into a must-have item, because it's a conscious choice as an expression of your individual style, or is worn 'ironically'. The only problem is that we are not in Year Twelve, we're in Year Ten!) I'm sure you can imagine the treatment meted out to anyone who looks like their mum still has a hand in their fashion choices. But for those who can't, let me spell it out for you: they will be snubbed, tarred, feathered, poisoned, drowned, burned at the stake, and stabbed. In a nutshell, their life at school will become a living hell. It's tantamount to pinning a sign to their backs saying 'Please Bully This Child'!

Yes, life isn't child's play, and everything has its consequences. Which brings us to the issue of underpants. I'm sure you'll remember, it was not long ago, how all male teenagers wore their underpants — or more precisely, their checked boxer shorts — on full display to the public, and their hair combed forwards across their face, causing a constant need to twitch their heads. And I hope you realise that all that is now over, and we can emerge from our hiding place behind our hair once more. The fringe-flicking twitch has now been replaced by the habit of running our fingers through our hair: the aim is not to sweep it into the face anymore, but to make it stand on end.

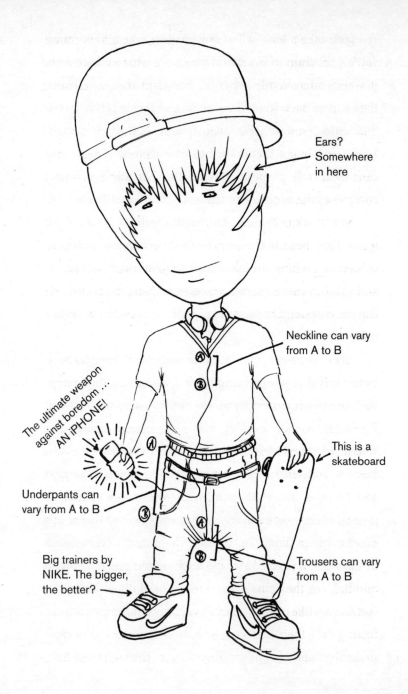

38

Just take a look at Justin Bieber, or take a look round you on the train to work, and you'll see what I mean. And, if you're interested in what happened to the underpants, they're now back where they belong — inside our trousers. That might sound pretty mainstream, but, to be honest, I never really got the whole boxers business. I mean, you can't even walk properly dressed like that, and running is completely out of the question.

But that's over now. And anyone who still hasn't got it into their head that the era of the checked boxers is over is literally inviting his classmates to give him a wedgie — and this can cause varying amounts of pain, depending on the victim's weight and stature. So, best keep those undies under wraps.

It's the same story with the fringe, which also goes back to Justin Bieber. Why Justin Bieber of all people should have such an influence on us guys is something I don't understand. Everyone says only girls like him, but a couple of years ago I suddenly found myself surrounded by miniature Justin Biebers. Trousers hanging down to their knees, hair longish and brushed into their faces. The importance of hair in general is completely over the top, anyway. The Bieber cut may have been ditched by its inventor himself — conquered by the side cut (shaved at the sides, long and gelled up in the middle), but the damage has already been done. Reflective surfaces act like magnets; boys won't leave the house without fussing over their hair first, and there are many who can't shake the habit of combing their fingers through their hair,

than boys, and all that. This leads to girls using make-up as young as twelve or thirteen (I don't have anything against make-up, in fact I love it — but at twelve?), and starting to wear skin-tight leggings, hot pants, low-cut T-shirts, T-shirts with holes in them that you can look through … All things I like to see, but am I allowed to like them, am I allowed to look?

'NO!!! Of course you're not, you fool!'

'Okay, sorry. I was only asking. But why do you dress like that then?'

'Stupid question!'

Is it really such a stupid question? I mean, most boys are looking for attention when they squeeze their torsos into ultra-tight T-shirts that display every muscle for public inspection. They want people to look. But it seems it's different for girls. They don't have a sixpack, not usually anyway — instead they have boobs and bums.

But only one person is allowed to look at a girl, and that's the person she likes at the moment. This marks the end of rational thought for boys; this is where chaos kicks in. Unfortunately, the girls' appearance triggers quite a reaction in teenage males. We've all been in the same biology classes, so there is some understanding of this behaviour. Boys who have just entered puberty can't stop making dirty comments and jokes about girls, or stop staring at their bums. Yet we can only expect a tirade of insults in response, and sarcastic questions like 'What do you want me to do, change the way I dress just for you?'

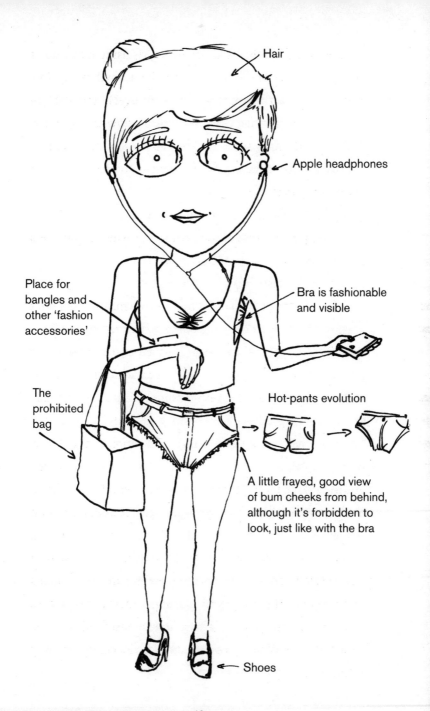

Hair

Apple headphones

Place for bangles and other 'fashion accessories'

Bra is fashionable and visible

The prohibited bag

Hot-pants evolution

A little frayed, good view of bum cheeks from behind, although it's forbidden to look, just like with the bra

Shoes

At least it's easier for us boys in winter, because that's when the girls haul their big scarves and baggy jumpers out of the wardrobe. But even then, some girls manage to find some see-through tights to put on that really show off everything they've got. Aren't they absolutely freezing? I'm already frozen to death and I'm wearing jeans! Maybe we underestimate the girls, and in fact they're much tougher than they look.

The question remains, do the girls do this on purpose to wind us boys up, or do they really not understand what effect they're having on us? I can't really believe either.

But then, what I really can't understand are the pornographic bags that some of the girls at my school have hanging from their arms. These feature pictures of shirtless guys, with the men shoving their hands down the front of their jeans. Again, I have nothing against pictures of good-looking men with their shirts off, but if a boy came to school with a bag that had a picture of a half-naked woman on it, he'd be dissed as a perv straightaway. Those exquisite bags are what you get when you buy a piece of clothing at Abercrombie & Fitch. Let's be magnanimous and gloss over the fact that simply entering one of those shops is an immoral act in itself, because the owner is such a total arsehole (who said in an interview in 2006 that he's only interested in selling his garments to people who are beautiful, thin, and rich). That doesn't seem to bother the girls at all. In fact, girls can get away with a load of stuff that boys can't even dream of doing.

Are there really no girls who are not like this? Can that really be all there is? Well, they do exist, but they're pretty damn thin on the ground. Fifteen-year-old girls with the confidence to look different are virtually non-existent in my school, unfortunately. There are just a couple of individuals who follow very different styles. I'm already looking forward to a time when we're all bigger (mentally, not physically), and it's easier for us to understand one another. I imagine we will, at least.

4

Drugs and Alcohol

or, what people are like when their
parents smoked weed and they grew
up watching a TV show where a chemistry
teacher runs a meth lab

If I believe everything my parents tell me, then the most contact they had with drugs was smoking a bit of weed. My mother's response to the drugs issue is to claim to have no use for them because she is naturally 'high on life'. Yeah, right, that's why we had to carry you home last New Year's Eve, as I remember, because you hadn't had anything to drink. Yes, Mum, alcohol is a drug, too.

From what I've learned, there are two kinds of drugs: the ones that make you addicted, and stupid, but 'cool' — sick, too, but not straight away; and then there are those that make you addicted, ugly, sick, unemployed, and eventually dead. The first group includes alcohol, cigarettes, weed, and coke. The second group covers heroin, morphine, and opium, as well as synthetic shit like ecstasy, krokodil, and crystal meth (the stuff they cook up in their campervan in *Breaking Bad*).

This is what I've managed to piece together from biology lessons, YouTube, *Breaking Bad*, and my parents. Not bad, eh? Once for a biology project at school, we each had to give a presentation on a drug, as a kind of 'know thine enemy' exercise. Needless to say, we all got a bit carried away and possessive about 'our' drug: 'My drug can cause psychoses!', 'Mine gets you addicted just from taking it once!', 'Mine shrinks your brain and turns you into a total dickhead!' This eventually descended into a massive argument about which drug was best and which was worst. What came out in the end was that the amount you take makes all the difference with every drug, and that you're never going to die of an overdose of weed or LSD. But who wants to end up spending their whole life with an expression like Dumbo or cringing with fear every time they see a bit of rubbish on the street?

Personally, I would not bow to peer pressure and take something just to look cool. So that counts out the drugs in the first group for me. And the second group I would never touch anyway. Our biology project ended with the teacher showing us an anti-drug film from the early eighties. There were actually a couple of scenes in it that really got under your skin — pretty disgusting and quite shocking: Those weird tight jeans that spread out at the bottom like a Native American teepee! And, whoa, man! ... The guys had high-heeled boots on! 'Did my parents walk round looking like that?' I wondered as I watched the movie. If they did, they're never going to live it down now!

As far as drug-taking went, I had thought I pretty much knew what to expect after what I'd seen in various shows on TV. But nothing and no one can prepare you for those blotchy, spotty faces and the shooting-up scenes. The girls were all, 'Eeeh-yuuuuck!!' The cool boys were like, 'Ha ha, LOL.' The other boys: 'Urghh, man!'

The film was crappy, but as a way of putting us off drugs by grossing us out, it was pretty effective.

Whenever I broach the subject of drugs, even in the slightest, with my dad, he always churns out the story of a good friend of his who died of an overdose. The first time he told it, I'll admit, I was shocked to hear something like that about an actual real person. But I've totally got the message now, and no amount of boring me with the same story can make the message any clearer. I've got it: drugs are shit, especially heroin.

With issues like drugs, I think adults just tend to err on the side of caution. They seem to think it's better to repeat something over and over a million times than say it once properly and clearly. That's a grown-up tactic I've never understood. If they keep droning on, at some point their nagging will have the opposite effect to the one they want! When my irritated father tells me ten times to have a shave, he only increases the probability that I won't do it, just to annoy him, even if I think the fuzz on my face looks ridiculous. Okay, I wouldn't start shooting up heroin just to irritate my dad, but, really, I don't need to hear the overdose story even one more time.

But forget heroin. There are two drugs that all people of my age have contact with, or most of us, at least: alcohol and weed. If I wanted to get hold of some marijuana, it would not be particularly difficult. I would just have to ask someone in my class or my year who I know sometimes smokes it to give me the number of their dealer, and … bam! You tell them how much you want to buy and set up a meeting. Just like in the gangster films, and astonishingly easy. Except that the guy doesn't have a flash car or a gun, but looks like any other bloke, although he might have the air of having been enjoying a bit too much of his own wares. But, as I said, I don't really know much about it, and what I do know came from friends.

Until recently, my experience of alcohol was about as extensive. Most people started going to parties where there was drink in Year Nine. The drink of choice was vodka from the outset, so I steered clear at first. I had often heard stories about a friend of a friend who ended up in hospital with alcohol poisoning, and that pretty much put me off the stuff. As did the media stories about people being given dodgy alcohol and going blind, or even dying, because their friends were scared to go and get help.

And anyway, I couldn't see the point of drinking something that tastes disgusting just to get drunk. And I'm afraid I still can't see the point. This means other people see me as some kind of alien, because everyone else seems to be really into it.

At one birthday party, someone smuggled in a bottle of vodka when the parents weren't too keen on the idea of a load of teenagers getting smashed in their house. Which is something I can fully understand — the parents' attitude, that is. There was Fanta and Coke at the party, too, and one person just had to show off by setting himself up as the cocktail expert. He just mixed everything up together and said it would be the perfect mixed drink. Which was bound to backfire, of course. I did try one or two sips. It wasn't particularly nice and the desired effect also failed to materialise … at first. It just burned a bit in my mouth.

The 'barman' became more and more euphoric with every plastic cup he served, as he couldn't resist tasting his concoction here and there. He nearly got alcohol poisoning and had to keep going to the toilet to puke. The rest of us didn't notice until he threw up all over our sleeping bags, keeled over, and went to sleep. At some point, someone heaved him into a clean bed and cleared up all the mess. Yum! And the best part was: the next morning, he couldn't remember a single thing. After that, I had even less desire to start drinking properly.

To be honest, the first hangover I ever had wasn't after a bout of binge drinking with my mates, but after going to a bar with my mother. We'd been to see the new Marvel movie with a friend of hers. I'm currently going through a superhero phase, so I have to keep finding people who will go to the cinema with me. Mum's always a willing cinema-chaperone, because there's nothing she likes better than to have someone explain films to her before, during, and after the screening. And I just happen to be an absolute specialist in the field of the superhero universe.

After the film, she wanted to go to a bar, and at first I was like, 'No way, they'll never let me in!' But then I got curious — I mean, please, who at my age has ever been into a bar? I was really nervous and stuff. From the inside, the bar looked exactly as I had imagined it, with music and dim lights. But the atmosphere was somehow friendly, and it was all totally new for me. And the cocktails were all so brightly coloured, with really cool decorations made out of fruit.

The first drink I chose was one with strawberries — it wasn't very strong and it tasted really nice. The second drink I picked was called a zombie and tasted pretty similar to the first. I had managed about half of what was quite a big glass before the alcohol hit me. It was a weird feeling — both numb and sharp at the same time. And everything seemed to be happening a little bit more slowly than normal, which was not a cool feeling, so I stopped drinking. Overall, the drinking experience was actually quite a kick. I might have suffered a slight hangover the next day, but somehow I've decided I like those brightly coloured beverages.

As I said, before that I had a lot of respect for strong alcohol, even fear. I found the mere idea that you could completely lose control of yourself if you're not careful to be pretty off-putting. But since nothing like that actually happened, I now see cocktails as pleasant, fun drinks whose effects are neither particularly appealing nor particularly appalling. You can have a good time and drink a little in the process, and maybe even enjoy it. Although I think the enjoyment comes a bit later. (This makes me sound like some old wine connoisseur, which I assure you I'm not. Wine tastes like shit!) Anyway, the result of my first bar experience was that I gained a more normal attitude to alcohol. I don't feel the urge anymore to run at the mere mention of the word vodka, and if I do drink, then it's out of a feeling of conviviality or something like that. So I don't drink much. Not enough to get smashed; just a bit.

When people in my class started drinking beer instead of vodka, I thought they had finally come to their senses. But no. At first, I was able to enjoy the odd beer with them at barbecue parties. But then came the drinking game we call 'beerball'.

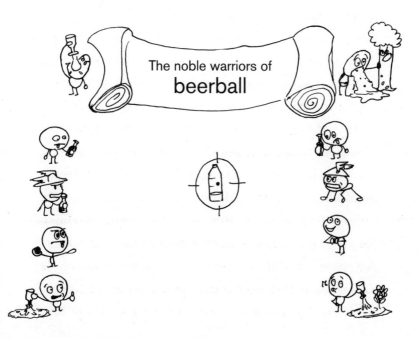

The noble warriors of
beerball

Played while watching football, beerball is a team game, and the winning team is the one whose members finish off their beer the fastest. But there is a slight sporting aspect to it, at least. The two teams stand facing each other, an empty bottle between them. The aim is to throw a ball at the empty bottle and knock it over — a bit like bowling. If the opposing team manages to knock the bottle over with the ball, you have to run over to it, stand it up again, and return to your position as fast as possible. The other team are allowed to drink from their beers for as long as that takes.

When we played it, most players had had enough after two rounds. The girls were tipsy, teetering across the lawn like drunken tightrope walkers, the boys couldn't stop burping, and everyone felt sick. Some had to be supported by a friend under each arm to stop them falling over all the time.

I may not have had any experience of speed drinking, but I can run fast and throw a ball, so I was quite a reasonable beerball player. My team lost the first round and won the second. Not least because another mate who has problems downing large amounts of beer in a small amount of time decided to seek out the shadows and water the garden with his beer. I was sorely tempted to follow suit, and that might have been the cleverest option. But my misplaced sense of fair play got the better of me, as it always does when there's a question of breaking the rules in a game. As I said, not very clever, but honourable at least.

After my third bottle of beer, it really was beginning to taste like shit, but luckily the game was almost over by then. We didn't really watch the football match, mainly because our team seemed to be losing for a while and we couldn't have faced a defeat. I was a bit drunk, like everyone else, but didn't feel particularly different, or strong, or great, or merry. I was just really tired and had more trouble than usual concentrating. Not particularly cool. So I think I'll stick to soft drinks for the time being, until I've figured out the point of drinking alcohol.

Anyway, my bar experience with my mum was a pretty cool introduction to the world of alcohol. But when she asked me recently if I wanted to smoke weed — that was really too much! I'm really not interested in having anything to do with that shit. And anyway, going to a bar is okay, even cool, but smoking dope with your own mother? I mean, that is a whole new level of cringe.

5

Computer Games

or, why gamers don't go on killing sprees

When the issue of computer games crops up, it usually means trouble. School grades plummet, daily chores don't get done, and there's constant arguing because a certain somebody won't stick to the agreed computer times. The daily scenario goes something like this:

Paul comes home from school with masses of homework to do, and would like to relax awhile with a computer game before tackling the mountain of work. As he goes to open the laptop, he notices his mother looking on disapprovingly.

'Paul, don't start playing computer games as soon as you come in! You haven't even said hello and you're already glued to that thing.'

Paul: 'Mum, please! I just need to relax for a bit.'

But Mum is sticking to her guns. 'Those games will rot your brain. Just put the computer away for now and pick your stuff up off the floor.'

Paul knows he'd better do as she says if he wants to get through the day in one piece. So he heaves himself off the couch and takes his stuff upstairs with a grumble. No sooner has he re opened the laptop than the whole thing starts again.

Mum: 'Will you please turn that game off now! I want to talk to you about something.'

Paul: 'Yeah, and I want to relax a little.'

Mum: 'Can't you see you're losing yourself in that artificial world? You're away at school the whole day, and when you *are* here, you're just stuck in front of that computer!'

An altercation like this can go on forever, and I know perfectly well what's coming next: the algebra test. It's all the fault of computer games that I failed that algebra test. It's computer games' fault that I'm always in a bad mood. In fact, anything negative at all can be blamed on them. That's pretty unfair towards computer games. If games had feelings, they would probably all be sad or angry at such mean accusations.

I know, parents just want to protect their children from bad things. But there are very few parents who actually take the time to really look at what their child is up to and what's really happening on that brightly coloured screen. Why waste time on something you know nothing about? When they think of gamers, most people imagine an overweight, pasty-faced boy who never leaves his room, has no mates, and lives in a world of his own. Until he goes to school one day and shoots everyone, and his classmates appear on the evening news saying all he ever did was play computer games.

To make it plain right from the start: none of my friends fit that description, not a single one. And these days, computer games are not all based on war. Just like music, books, or films, games come in different genres. There are browser games, RPGs (role-playing games), action games, strategy games, life simulations, and so on, and so on. Some games are more fun to play than others. Some cost money; others are free. Some are about shooting people, ogres, goblins, pigs, birds, insects, spaceships, or, of course, aliens; others are about building your own little village.

I, for one, spent at least a year tending a virtual farm on Facebook. Yes, I played *Farmville* … I'm not ashamed to admit it! A friend of mine asked me via Facebook if I could help him harvest his wheat or something like that. And before I knew it, I had a virtual farm of my own on my hands. *Farmville* is a social-network game — played with others via the internet or Facebook — and free, at first. There are various scenarios in social-network games: you have to look after a farm, or run a hotel or restaurant or something similar, construct your own ancient or medieval city, command a spaceship … stuff like that.

So, I had my own farm. At first, it was no more than just four small vegetable patches, but under my care it expanded to include fields, animals, and a barn. I sowed, harvested, and sowed again. Soon, I had fixed times when my produce was ripe for harvesting and new crops had to be sown. I would come home from school and settle on the couch with the computer on my knee to harvest my corn in time so I could exchange it for play money. After not too long, I had enough to afford a small cherry orchard, a pond, five cats (they were very rare and expensive, and they also moved around!), and even a hot-air balloon. At Halloween, by the way, there were also flesh-eating plants and pumpkins to play with.

But the thing is, while you're 'working' your arse off to 'earn' all that play money, other players simply buy it with real money, so they can afford much cooler stuff. Then you realise that you can actually buy more or less everything in this game. And soon you're thinking whether buying a thing or two would really make that big a dint in your pocket-money budget. Of course, you can carry on playing for free, but your farm will never be as cool as those run by people spending real money. One friend of mine, for example, did decide to invest some real money in his farm. He had everything you could imagine: at least twenty cats, a field that was four times the size of mine, hot-air balloons, villas, a swimming pool, a beach, Halloween-edition trees, haunted castles … At some point, you're so frustrated by such inequality that you either stop playing or start spending real money on the game.

Spending money on a farm, a stupid virtual farm on the internet!?? No thanks, I thought, and stopped playing *Farmville*. And anyway, I was starting to get sick of having to harvest my fucking wheat at the same time every day.

Still, it seems crazy how much time I spent on that game when I think about it now. For an entire year, I wasted at least half an hour a day on it. But if my mother had banned me from playing it, I would not have seen why. It took time, but eventually I realised for myself that I should be spending my time on other things.

So far, I've played three games like that, and with each new game I had more control over myself and was able to stop playing more easily. So, overall, I'd say games like that are pretty harmless, as long as you don't go overboard spending money on them.

Recently, I decided to have a look at my old vegetable garden, but it's disappeared somehow. Shame. And that's another problem: games don't last forever, and some simply get closed down without so much as a by-your-leave. For what reason, no one knows. Then there you sit, having lost everything, your entire vegetable garden. And to make matters worse, even your virtual cats are dead.

Just as social-network games are pretty harmless, so are fantasy role-playing games — or 'felt-hat games', as my father likes to call them, which comes from the fact that most fantasy RPGs are rooted in the *Lord of the Rings* books. But from those origins, they've morphed into a huge hodgepodge of fantasy worlds. In the *Elder Scrolls* series, the elves alone are divided into dozens of races: Dark Elves, Wood Elves, Blood Elves, High Elves … I can't keep track of any more than that. But I think the Blood Elves and the

High Elves are enemies. The typical premise of a felt-hat game goes something like this: defend your land from the evil hordes of the dark shadow of Blah Blah Blah; only you can find the sword of light and, with its help, restore peace in your realm. None of the characters are ever called just 'Paul', but always something like 'Paul, son of Robert, kinsman of Yadda Yadda Yadda, and mightiest warrior of the northern latitudes'. (Okay, that was a bit over the top, but you know what I mean.)

Anyway, you can certainly get as absorbed in these games as you can in a good fantasy novel. (Though perhaps I shouldn't say this. I read and read and can't stop until my eyelids droop with tiredness. Not particularly conducive to paying attention in class the next day at school.)

The other important question is whether outright bans on playing computer games do any good at all. In my case, for example, I wasn't allowed to play computer games until I got to high school. But when I finally was allowed and started playing them, I had hardly any self-control and spent entire days lost in those fantasy worlds. Friends of mine who were allowed to start playing them earlier had much more control over their own gaming behaviour. It's the direct opposite of smoking: the earlier you start smoking, the more difficult it is to give up; with computer games, the risk of addiction tends to go down, the longer you play them.

That's why I find it difficult to say what the best age is for a child to be allowed to play computer games. I think the general rule is: as long as you are not neglecting your friends and hobbies for the sake of a game, and at least occasionally put in a bit of school work, gaming is unlikely to pose a danger.

In fact, I've only ever met one boy who was really addicted to gaming. But he was having huge problems at school, and his parents had no time for him because his father was seriously ill. The fact that he never wanted to emerge from his computer-generated world was something even I could understand.

Another thing adults often get wrong is to assume that gaming turns you into a loner.

First of all, games alone cannot do anything. It's all in the hands of the player and his attitude to the game. I find it hard to believe that someone with a sociable character would suddenly turn into an outsider because of a computer game. On the other hand, I can imagine that someone dealing with serious social problems might want to shut themselves off from the world by gaming. That kind of thing is really fucked up, but it's not the game's fault.

On the contrary — games can be social. More social than reading books, at any rate. Nearly all computer games have a multiplayer mode that lets you play with or against friends, who might be in the same room or elsewhere, via a network. Because of this, gaming is simply a part of life for our generation. Anyone thinking of not allowing their child to play should maybe keep that in mind.

One such multiplayer game, for example, is *League of Legends* (or *LoL* for short). It's a fantasy multiplayer free-to-play game, which means you can download it via the internet for free and then play it with your friends online.

People who play *LoL* don't just disappear into a fantasy world of their own for hours on end, although they do talk to each other as if they came from another planet, which means their conversation is unintelligible to normal human beings even if it isn't actually in a foreign language. So don't be surprised when you read the conversation below, which was written by a good friend of mine who's an active *LoL* player.

A: 'Yo! How many LPs have you got at the moment?'

B: '42. I won two rounds coz I had the coolest killing sprees.'

A: 'I have 78. I was in promo, but I had too many feeders on my team.'

B: 'It's the flamers that are really annoying. They ruin your chances of any teamwork.'

A: 'Yeah, it's shit when that happens. Have you seen the new champ? That guy's so OP. His ult can take out a whole opposing team.'

B: 'So, Riot should definitely nerf him. Anyway, they shouldn't just keep revealing new champs, they should develop new skins instead.'

A: 'No way. It's shitty that skins cost RPs anyway. As if I'd spend good money just to look different!'

B: 'But then the champs look really epic and it's not a pay-to-win, coz you don't get any buffs, you just change your appearance.'

A: 'Well, I never buy skins, but you can try them out on the PBE. The only problem is that there are so many trolls there.'

B: 'Server is pretty full of lurking newbies who don't even know what pings are.'

A: 'Yeah, they don't communicate with the team, and flamers are the opposite. But it's best not to mute them, at least not in a ranked. Sometimes they do come up with something useful.'

B: 'Muting's a bad idea in rankeds, but you have to in normals. If you just wanna enjoy the game, mute 'em all and turn off cross-team chat.'

Here's a translation of this conversation for the uninitiated:

A: 'A good day to you, sir. How is your game progressing?'

B: 'Greetings to you, too. I have now been victorious in two games in succession, by virtue of the fact that I eliminated a large number of players in a short space of time. My performance was rewarded with 42 league points.'

A: 'I had a number of very important games, which could have enabled me to rise within the league system. However, unfortunately, my fellow players were too weak, thus allowing our opponent to gain in strength. I achieved an evaluation of only 78 points.'

B: 'Well, there is nothing one can do in such a situation. However, some players spend a great deal of time writing unhelpful comments, making it rather difficult to communicate sensibly with the rest of one's fellow players. This makes acting as a consolidated unit nigh-on impossible.'

A: 'I have also experienced such players in a team of mine. It is extremely vexing. Are you familiar with the newest game character, by the way? He is able to eliminate an entire opposing team with his strongest attack. He is so incredibly powerful!'

B: 'The developers of this game should not keep introducing new characters, but rather create new guises for existing characters. Furthermore, they should weaken the new character, for the sake of fairness.'

A: 'I am not of the same opinion, above all because I am not prepared to pay good money simply to change the appearance of an existing character.'

B: 'As I see it, a new guise lends a character a greater air of strength and power, despite the fact that the new appearance has no effect on a character's abilities.'

A: 'Still, I do not purchase them, since one may "try them on" in the game's testing area. The only problem is that the players there do not take the game seriously and often die deliberately, rendering it impossible to play a proper game.'

B: 'There are, however, also players on the main servers who are simply incapable. They do not place signals on the map and so do not warn others of the whereabouts of opponents, or they fail to inform others when they lose track of an opponent.'

A: 'Precisely, and they do not use the chat system properly to communicate with their team. Others, by contrast, make too much use of the chat facility, constantly writing nonsense. However, they should not be silenced, at least not during important league games, since they may eventually communicate something that is of use.'

B: 'Indeed, I am of the same opinion; however, during less important games, the best strategy is to mute such players and to turn off the chatting facility in order to have more fun.'

As far as killing and massacring are concerned, *LoL* is totally harmless. Mostly, it's just a few colourful characters walking through enchanted forests and meadows, attacking each other with medieval weapons or magic. It has absolutely nothing in common with so-called killer games or shoot-'em-ups.

My first experience of a first-person shooter game was in Year Five. Suddenly, it seemed like everyone had an iPod Touch. Everyone except me, of course, because my parents refused to buy me one. Everyone else was using their iPod Touch to play a game called *Modern Combat 2: Black Pegasus*. It was a first-person shooter with pistols, machine guns, and rocket launchers. As you increased your rank, you unlocked new weapons, until you had the best weapon of all: a golden AK-47. Maximum precision and minimum recoil. The thing that made this game so popular was that you could play it via Bluetooth or wi-fi, so several people could play against each other, or with each other, at the same time. In winter, when people's iPod batteries were particularly quick to run out, a crowd of shivering penguins would form around the final fighters, eagerly following the progress of the game. I can even remember one birthday party where everyone was sitting around in different parts of the living room, all with an iPod in their lap, cursing when they got hit by one of those damn snipers.

Some games that are much more violent than that include *Assassin's Creed*, *Call of Duty*, *Grand Theft Auto*, and *Outlast*.

Call of Duty is one of those games that the phrase 'shoot-'em-up' must have been invented for. It's a pure war game, and you normally only play online with friends. It has a story arc, but the plot is totally irrelevant, and few people are interested in who it is they're shooting at and why. This is the kind of game you keep on playing until you get bored of it, or the next game in the series comes out. A phase like that can extend over a few months, and nearly every day you arrange with your friends to log on at the same time, each at home in his own room. Sometimes, someone goes offline mid-game, which usually means he's not actually allowed to play this kind of game and a parent has come in. But you just keep on playing and then argue about who was best the next morning at school.

Once, a friend of mine borrowed an action-adventure-survival-horror game called *The Last of Us*. It was great! Horror games are a relatively new genre. Usually, you're unarmed, and, like the characters in a horror movie, you find yourself stuck in a nightmarish situation. Talk about 'frightfully' cool! Most of the time we played it from the perspective of a guy called Joel, whose family had been killed by zombies and who now had to look after Ellie, a girl the same age as his dead daughter. It was like a cross between a game and a blockbuster movie.

We played it in our living room, much to my mother's annoyance. We played it late into the night, and the next morning we carried on from where we'd left off. First, we had to sneak past a load of zombies — I didn't realise they were undead at first, so I just opened fire on them with my gun. But soon I worked out what to do, and managed to knife a few quietly without their cronies noticing. Eventually, we had to face a Bloater — an old, fat, fungus-covered zombie giant. It took us hours to finish off that snot-spouting bastard.

Paul: 'He won't die, the fucker!'

Francis: 'Shoot him in the head, quick!'

Paul: 'I am! It's not working!!!' (Bloater starts to make weird noises.) 'Great, *now* the revolting thing's just standing there.' (Bloater spits a huge snot-ball at Joel.)

Francis: 'Shoot!!'

Paul: 'I am! Fuck, what's it doing now?!!!'

Francis: '… aaarghh …'

Paul: 'It's …'

Francis: 'You've …'

Paul: 'He's just killed Joel!!!'

Francis: 'Man, this Bloater!'

It was a pretty full-on game. Me and Francis still talk about it now, sometimes. In a strange way, that scary experience created a bond between us. Ah yes, the Bloater, those were the days!

So experiences like that turn people into lone wolves or high-school shooters, do they? If that was the case, almost all the boys in my class would have already gone on high-school shooting sprees or at least have attacked someone with their fists. And: wouldn't films, books, and comics have the same effect?

Okay, it's true that the first-person perspective of some of these games makes them seem more real than a book written in the first person. But, still, under normal circumstances, everything that happens in a game stays in the game. We teenagers are able to distinguish between reality and a game. It does sometimes happen that someone can get aggressive after playing a game, if it was particularly nerve-wracking, or if he lost. But that's just a normal expression of frustration, just like some people might smash their racquet in rage after losing a tennis match. Violent games are as likely to turn you into a homicidal maniac rampaging through high school as *Farmville* is to turn you into a peace-loving agriculturalist.

6

Sex and Porn

or, why there's still room for
just holding hands

Just after the start of Year Five, we were in the school gym and suddenly all my classmates were using words like gay, straight, homo, and trans.

Maurice: 'Man, Leo, you homo, stop getting in my way, will you?'

Leo: 'I can't help it — there's hardly any room on my side! Anyway, do you even know what "homo" means?'

Maurice: 'Err, course I do, "homo" means "gay".'

Eavesdropping on this conversation, Paul's interest is piqued.

Paul: 'What's "gay"?'

Leo: 'Are you serious, Paul?'

Maurice: 'You don't know what "gay" means?'

Now I felt like a total idiot. Maybe everyone else really did know what they were talking about, but I doubt it somehow. When I asked my parents about those words, they were pretty surprised. And I suddenly felt a bit too young for my age. I mean, not long before, in primary school, we were still colouring in pictures of jolly, grinning sperms and labelling diagrams with such lovely words as 'uterus', 'ovum', 'spermatozoon', and 'embryo'. Now, suddenly, everybody seemed to be an expert on how the whole business worked.

This was annoying. Much more embarrassing, though, were the attempts my parents then kept making to casually explain the 'birds and bees' to me. Sometimes they would suddenly launch into one when I was least expecting it, making me want to stick my fingers in my ears and blow a loud whistle to drown out their voices. Just moments before, we might have been chatting about the most trivial of matters, and suddenly my dad would nervously clear his throat and say:

'Erm, Paul …

'… you might recently have started feeling the need to …

'… it's completely normal to sometimes …

'… everything's fine, I'm sure, but if your penis starts hurting, you must …

'… there's no need to feel ashamed, it's perfectly normal to wake up in the morning with …'

I would try to change the subject, talk about the weather, even school. Finally, they had mercy and — secretly, so my younger brother wouldn't know about it — gave me a cool (this is very important: actually cool and not wannabe-cool) book. And that was it, job done. Those of you who are too embarrassed to ask the bookseller at your local bookshop for advice about publications of this nature should just go for the book *Sex & Lovers*. It really helped me cope with this difficult, confusing period in my life ... No, but seriously, it's a good book. It tells you a lot about kissing and cuddling, and about the fact that stimulating a woman's genitals takes more than just working through a repertoire of gymnastic positions the way they do in porn. Or that it's okay if your erect penis doesn't have the dimensions of a medieval pole-axe.

Just to dash any hopes you might still have right now: yes, by Year Seven, or Year Nine at the very latest, every boy has watched porn! It's not easy for boys. Or for girls, either, I know. But as a boy, from the time puberty kicks in, you only have one thing on your mind, and one thing in your hand. I mean, if someone gives you a totally cool new toy that can do all sorts of tricks, you're going to want to play with it, aren't you? You used to have a puny little thing that didn't really do much at all, then you get a mega-upgrade and — BAM! — suddenly it can do all these great things. And then there are the hormones, which are at least as much to blame for our inability to think straight or resist the urge to check out certain websites. Yes, I blame the hormones!

One way or another, you're bound to end up at one of those bright-pink websites with lots and lots of videos on them. The variety of categories is almost endless, from MILFs (Mothers I'd Like to Fuck) to BBWs (Big Beautiful Women). Some guys in my class once had the brilliant idea of watching a porn video, featuring the consumption of faeces, in the computer room. Six months later, a furious, and of course disappointed, headmaster stormed into our classroom — disappointed, probably because he had not expected such behaviour from kids in Year Six. So whether you watch them with friends, are shown them by your best mate, are sent them via chat, or search for them yourself — sooner or later, everyone comes into contact with this dark force.

Protecting your child from this is possible only to a certain extent, especially if he (or possibly she) is better at using computers than you are. I think talking openly about porn is the only strategy that makes any sense. Or give your offspring the aforementioned book.

To be perfectly honest, I don't know whether girls are interested in pornography or not. But whenever girls see boys watching porn on their phones, or even hear boys talking about it — usually the most bizarre and disgusting sort — the ensuing screaming is pretty ear-splitting. Then come the disgusted faces, patronising or pert comments, and so on. There is one scientific study that says girls watch porn, too. But girls are either very good at keeping such viewing habits a secret or the 'study' is just one of the ones that somebody made up.

I would actually like to lead a discussion in our ethics class on the problematic question of whether and to what extent watching porn fucks you up. This might sound like a recipe for social suicide, but at least it would give us boys a chance to explain ourselves. What is actually the problem, if some people prefer to imagine scenes in their head, and others need a visual aid? One is creative and imaginative, and the other, well … Some people believe we've lost the ability to use our imaginations to conjure up pleasant scenes because porn has filled our heads with shit. I think you forget the shit pretty quickly, luckily, and there is still room for holding hands and lying next to each other, rather than on top of each other. I would be happy just for the opportunity to have a cup of tea with the girl of my dreams, to talk to her and laugh with her, or even just be with her.

And this brings us to another issue, one which is much more complicated than sex. I think it's difficult to have a proper conversation with someone about being 'in love'. We teenagers are well aware that being in love is one of the best feelings in the world — even if we would never put it that way. In fact, we usually used the word 'like' instead of 'in love with', because it sounds less momentous. It's a simplification, but it also downgrades the issue and makes it feel less embarrassing/difficult to talk about.

Of course, the last thing you want is for word to get around that you like someone. So, at school, you have to take care not to leap to a girl's aid too often when she's being set upon by rowdy or randy classmates. Otherwise, others might notice you like her, and it would be over before it has even begun. So you can only turn to your best friend — if to anyone at all — for advice. You compare impressions of the person in question, fret about choosing the perfect birthday present for her, or worry about how to even start a conversation with her.

Every shitty WhatsApp or Facebook message you send her is fraught with insecurity about whether you've chosen just the right words, or some other tiny detail. And when she doesn't respond within seconds, you imagine she's busy texting with someone else, or she's deliberately ignoring you and you can do nothing but stare at your phone in desperation. Every damn second is filled with weird fantasies where you're the hero impressing her with your prowess, or you're off on an exciting adventure together. And, for example, if the train you're on happens to pass through her neighbourhood, your insides get all churned up at the thought that she might happen to get on your train at any moment — and when she doesn't, you're devastated. But, needless to say, all this is top secret. At least, you try your best to keep it secret.

What follows is a typical conversation: Paul and Tom on their way home from school. Tom reckons he's worked out that Paul likes Anna.

Tom: 'There's no need to be embarrassed about it, mate, I'm sure she likes you, too.'

Paul: 'Man, Tom! How many times do I have to tell you? I just think she's nice, that's all. Okay? Drop it, dude!'

Tom won't drop it: 'And why are you always meeting up with her, then? Eh??'

Paul: ''Cause I find her easy to talk to — unlike you!'

Tom knows he's almost achieved his aim: 'Talking, is that all?? Dude, you're such a killjoy! Haven't you even kissed her yet, or … ?' (Tom makes very unmistakable gestures; Paul can't help grinning, despite himself.)

Paul: 'Shut up, you spaz! No, and I don't even want to kiss her, man. We're just really good friends, I don't want to risk losing that.'

Tom: 'Uh-oh — the boy's been friendzoned!! Hard luck, mate! Sorry, there's nothing you can do now. Happens to the best of us. Only to the best of us.' (Gives Paul a pitying look.)

Paul: 'Huh? What's that supposed to mean — "friendzoned"? What is that?'

Tom: 'That, my young padawan, means so close you are, and yet so far, from what you desire.'

Paul: 'What are you on about, man?'

Tom: 'You're like a gay best friend, no danger, and so of no interest when it comes to certain things.'

Paul: 'But I'm not gay. And what "certain things" are you talking about?'

Tom: 'You know very well what I'm talking about.'

Paul: 'For fuck's sake, I don't even want to kiss her.'

Tom: 'Sure, that's what you tell me. Weird, 'cause she's always looking at you in that funny way. I could have sworn ...'

Paul (hopefully): 'She what? Stop taking the piss now. As if she ... Does she really do that?'

Tom: 'Now you mention it, she was asking after you yesterday when you were off school.'

Paul: 'She was what? Tom, stop pissing around! As if she'd ask about me!'

Tom: 'She did, really, I swear!'

Paul: 'Look me in the eyes ... Ha! See, you're smiling. You're the worst liar ever!!!'

Tom: 'Alright, don't believe me, then. I can't help being a smiley person.'

Paul (bursting with joy): 'And what can I do about being friendzoned? How can I get out of the zone?'

Tom: 'Sorry, man, but there's no hope, I'm afraid. I bet

you even chat with her parents.'

Paul: 'What's that got to do with anything?'

Tom: 'If her parents like you, you can forget it, at least at our age. If they like you, they say stuff like "Why don't you go out with Paul, his school grades are so good and he's such a nice young man ..." and before you know it, she's associating you with all those negative things. She wants to get on her parents' nerves and she can't use you to do that. Too polite, too nice.'

Paul: 'I always thought that being nice was a good thing.'

Tom: 'Yeah, it is, later, when you want to get married, but not now. Girls of our age go for posers; arseholes; lying, macho, antisocial potheads; drinkers; and bad boys. Like me, for instance.'

Whether girls have similar conversations, I have no idea. They're even more secretive, but I expect they're not so different from us boys. Maybe they have even more far-out fantasies, with horses and vampires or something. Did you know the guy who plays the werewolf in *Twilight* has a girl's name? Yes, 'he' is called Taylor Lautner. Which I think is pretty funny, but there are a couple of things us boys had better not make fun of, and, yes, as I mentioned before, *Twilight* is one of them. That's something you just don't do. *You don't mess with* Twilight*!!!* You just don't. You don't mess with *Twilight*, just like you don't make fun of boy bands, actors, or cute pop stars. If you do, the girls will be down on you like a ton of bricks within seconds, and they don't forget quickly. Tom and I experienced this first hand when we slagged off a certain rapper's look. If it wasn't for some traitors within the girls' ranks, I probably wouldn't be here now to tell the tale.

That's one of the things girls can't take a joke about. But some things aren't so bad. For example, you can snatch a girl's homework book, or pinch her phone to search it for interesting messages. Girls see stuff like that as welcome attention. If you steal their homework book and leaf through it, she'll say something like 'Hey, man, give me my book back!' But really, she's pleased. A boy stole my homework book! That's like a public proposal of marriage. Well, almost. Stealing her phone is even better, because then she assumes the boy is interested in her chats with other people, which might be the case, or it might not.

In any case, you can't give her her phone back straightaway, not till you've properly teased her first. Not until she has endured that will she get her phone back. That's the way it was back in Year Five, and that's the way it remains in Year Ten. But I don't do any phone-snatching, for two clear reasons: I, personally, would not like it if someone took my phone. And if you break it, you've really had it. No matter how much the girls like the attention. So take care when using this method!

Another thing you have to be careful with is public appreciation of girls' secondary sexual characteristics. Irrespective of whether the opinion you voice is positive or negative, it will almost always be unwelcome. And always be on your guard — the walls have ears!

Despite Tom's advice, I am always friendly, thoughtful, polite, and helpful — a gentlemen. Or a boring killjoy. 'Boring' is a very, very bad word. Girls you don't know much about because they hardly say anything are usually labelled 'boring'.

And this brings us to a favourite activity of boys: rating girls. No, not everyone has their own tastes. Usually, a girl counts as hot or not for the majority of the group. For example:

A group of boys are sitting on the sports field, feeling bored. Suddenly, Carla from our class walks by. She's bought herself a new pair of shoes. And she's wearing false eyelashes.

Maurice: 'Aw, no, man, take a look at those shoes! How trashy does she look?!'

Leo: 'Dude, why would anybody buy shoes like that? And those eyelashes, they look so cheap!'

Maurice: 'Does she think she looks hot in those hot pants? It's so gross, you can see everything she's got!'

Bart: 'But her friend Helen, she's really hot, have you seen her pics on Facebook?'

Leo: 'Is she the one with the massive tits?! Phwoar, man, she's so fit.'

Maurice: 'I dunno what you see in her, she's got gross hair.'

Leo: 'Nah, man, she's fit!!'

Bart: 'Shut it, Maurice, you don't know what you're talking about!'

Maurice: 'I've just got class, that's all.'

Bart: 'Hey, douche, who do you think's hot, then?'

Maurice: 'You know that girl in our year, the one who was going out with the guy from Year Twelve who's always standing outside the gates, smoking?'

Bart: 'You mean Leah? You're right, she's got great legs.'

Leo: 'Leah? She's totally flat-chested. Absolutely boobless.'

I don't think rating other human beings in this way is particularly cool. It's a pretty arrogant thing to do, to look down on people just to make yourself feel superior. But it's not only the boys who are bad that way — girls can be incredibly full of themselves, too. Boys who are younger than them are usually on their shit list automatically. Which shouldn't actually apply to me, because I'm a year older than most people in my class. But even that's not enough, because some girls actually really believe that they are far, far ahead of us, intellectually. Which I, incidentally, have my doubts about.

Tom sometimes tells tall stories about parties he's been to. He says he nearly slept with a girl, but she had to leave early, and he lost her number. Yeah, right.

Nothing like that went on at parties I've been to. Most people are too embarrassed to even dance. They prefer to get drunk, and if any kissing does go on, it feels like back in primary school, when everything was so exciting and new. There's a lot of fuss, but it's usually forgotten by the next day. Of course, there are boys who'll try to make a pass at any girl who's too drunk to know what she's doing, but her friends are usually there to protect her.

This makes it sound like all boys are just evil arseholes. Somehow, we always end up looking like the bad guys when it comes to sex and relationships. But you have to remember, we're still trying to find a way through this minefield. That's how I see it, anyway. You shouldn't have to hide the fact that you're in love, but you do have to be able to accept it when the object of your desires doesn't return the sentiment (and her friends take the piss out of you). They say it's no longer up to us boys to make the first move, but, somehow, that's still what people expect. And if it should work out, then the entire relationship has to be conducted in public, otherwise the girl will think you're embarrassed to be her boyfriend.

Such things can put an end to a relationship before it's even begun. Both people might be head-over-heels in love with each other, but if they don't have the courage to show it, nothing will ever come of it and they can keep on dreaming. I know that it's always better to do something than nothing, but it's still hard to have the courage of your convictions. Being honest to others and to yourself isn't an easy thing to do.

7

School

or, why it would be better if some teachers were a bit more like the meth-cooking chemistry teacher from Chapter 4

There are some days when nothing seems to go right. You oversleep, don't have time for a shower, just manage to get to school in time — and as soon as you spot your teacher, you realise he's had a bad night's sleep, too, and would rather be doing anything other than teaching your class right now. He scrawls something or other on the board, comments on it briefly and tells you to open your books; individual work. After ten minutes, the whole class is getting bored and fidgety, and most start chatting or looking at their phones secretly under their desks.

Suddenly, the teacher looms in front of you, and wants to know why you're talking when you haven't even finished half the work he set. And there you are, looking like a dickhead, while everyone else pretends they've finished their work. You're left with a black mark against your name, and you're called up to the board to explain a formula you've definitely never seen before; clearly the teacher wants to make an example of you.

Rather than coming to your aid, your classmates stab

you in the back, raising their hands and whimpering to be called to give the answer, while the teacher looks down on you pityingly, smug in the knowledge that he's achieved his aim of showing you up in front of all your friends and the nicest girl in the class. Eventually, the teacher saves one of your classmates from death by arm ache. Proud and excited, the chosen one spouts the solution, and the teacher rewards him — like a trained dog that gets a treat for performing a trick — with a satisfied nod of acknowledgement.

Finally, you're allowed to return to your desk, and you spend the rest of the lesson in inner truancy, refusing to participate in class. When the bell goes for break time and everyone is gathering up their belongings and making for the door, you hang back, alone, because you don't particularly feel like spending time with your arsehole classmates. When half the class has already left, the teacher writes on the board, 'Major vocab test tomorrow! Pages 189 to 200, plus grammar points 34/35.' And you know that no one except for the usual swots will study for the test, and that your choice is either a ruined afternoon spent revising vocab, or an 'F'.

And anyway, why would someone wait till half the class has left to write the homework up on the board?

Different teachers have different methods of administering their dose of homework. Some teachers believe that a board half-filled with closely written text represents the perfect workload, while others usually just ask you to review the lesson at home so it stays in your head for a while at least. Then there are those who would prefer to let students teach themselves the new material, with the aid of Wikipedia. So what do you do when you have teachers from all four of those schools of thought on one day? How are you supposed to manage all that?

The answer is simple: group chat. The way this works is that each student who's willing takes on part of the homework load, photographs it, and uploads the pic via group chat for others to copy. And the next day, everyone has all their homework completed. You have to be careful not to copy other people's homework word for word. Once everyone has handed in their work, if the teacher realises you've been copying, all parties will automatically fail straightaway, or get an 'F to go' as some witty teachers like to call it.

What most teachers don't seem to realise is that theirs is not the only, or even the most important, subject in school. A short research question might be manageable as homework, but when you've also got a debate to prepare for, and an essay to write for ethics class, and quadratic equations to solve for algebra, and you're at school anyway till half past three in the afternoon, followed by sports training, it may well be the case that you don't feel like sitting down at ten o'clock to face some physics problems — particularly when you didn't understand them in the lesson anyway.

My usual tactic is to study ahead only as far as the next test. By the time a test is marked and handed back, I've already forgotten so much that I only recognise about half the questions, if that. I'm now in Year Ten, which means I've spent more years at school than most people spend working in one job. If I ask myself how much of all that learning I've actually retained, the answer has to be: not very much. I can do addition, subtraction, multiplication, and division; use a calculator; read and write, although spelling's not exactly my strong point, and neither is punctuation (my teacher says I throw punctuation marks at the text by the fistful, like a sower broadcasting his seed); and I'm also pretty good at solving for x in algebra, but something tells me I'll forget this skill pretty quickly once I've left school.

What else? I know how to play volleyball and basketball, which I'm sure will come in handy in later life. In history, I've learned how to cite a historical source and assess its reliability, and I've learned a large chunk of our country's history. In philosophy, I was totally confused by Descartes' proof of the existence of God, but I did think the allegory of the cave was pretty cool. I'm also able to categorise logical arguments, such as … Damn it, I've forgotten! But I can still argue reasonably well. I'm also able to make a presentation using PowerPoint — I actually think that's a good skill, because I'll probably need to make PowerPoint presentations later in life.

I'm sure I could name a few more skills I've picked up if I thought about it for long enough. But the fact that I would have to rummage around in my mind to find them is shocking in itself. Ten years. Why am I forced to learn so much by rote, when I just forget it again straightaway? Maybe that's the point of school, to get you used to the fact that a lot of the work you have to do in life is neither fun nor useful. Why do we all have to study maths, when only two people in my class are interested in it and the rest have to really struggle to get our heads round something we're guaranteed never to need again?

And why did we have only two years of classes on how to use applications like PowerPoint and Word? And what about computer programming? Okay, maybe the teachers don't know enough about that kind of stuff to teach us, but why don't they get someone in who does? Woodwork and metalwork, cooking, sewing — that's all missing from the curriculum at high schools like mine. Performing arts and sports are the only two lessons on the timetable that offer students any respite.

I'd rather spend my time doing something that I believed would help me get on in life. And, if the system won't let me specialise, I'd at least like to know what I need all this knowledge for. They don't need to explain why it's useful, but I want to know what it is about a given subject that's supposed to be so great, how it fits in to the grand scheme of things, life beyond school, in the outside world. It's not much help when the first thing a teacher tells you is that he's never needed algebra since he left school himself.

It's not that I expect teachers to go completely crazy in lessons and jump up on the desk like Jack Black in *School of Rock*, although that would be pretty cool — no, it would be more than enough if teachers could inject a certain enthusiasm into their lessons that rubs off on their students. In *Breaking Bad*, there's a scene where the terminally ill chemistry teacher Walter White, who later sets up a meth lab in his RV, is explaining to his class why chemistry is so important. Listening to those few lines of script was the first time I understood what someone might find so fascinating about chemistry.

'Chemistry is the study of matter, but I prefer to see it as the study of change ... Electrons, they change their energy levels ... Molecules change their bonds. Elements, they combine and change into compounds ... That's all of life, right? ... It's the constant, it's the cycle, it's solution, dissolution, just over and over and over. It is growth, then decay, then transformation. It is fascinating, really.'

After that episode, I had the feeling for the first time that chemistry could actually be a really interesting subject, although I'd already been taking it for two years. With just a little bit more encouragement, I might even have done more of my chemistry homework.

The best thing is when teachers tell us stories from their own experience. It's just much more genuine when someone speaks from personal experience, and that makes it easier to remember. For example, we once had a police officer who came to talk to our class. He told us the story of a man who was stabbed and killed when he tried to intervene in a fight. The policeman said that that man would probably still be alive today if he had known what we were about to be told — and then he explained how to react and keep safe if you are mugged or attacked.

I can still remember it to this day. The first rule is: run

away. The second rule is: run away. The third rule is: if you can't run away, hand over everything they want and don't do anything stupid.

Definitely never carry a knife, because you're more likely to end up getting stabbed with it than your attacker. No matter how big and strong or good at karate you are, you can't block blades or bullets. Then he told us a few cops 'n' robbers stories. Best double period ever! We didn't want to let him out of the classroom.

But school is not normally as educational as that. It's still cool though, because it's where you get to see your friends every day. You have the daily drudge of lessons, but at least you have other people to share your ordeal with. It needn't be your best friend who you bitch about the last lesson with, but, whoever it is, you know they're someone who feels the same way you do. And sometimes the last lesson of the day is cancelled and we go out and play football, and maybe a teacher might even join in, and pass the ball to you at a critical time in the game, and you score. At moments like that, the past is forgotten, old rivals pat each other on the back, teachers see a different side of their students — and vice versa, of course. In general, if you occasionally do stuff together that doesn't have to do with lessons, you get on better with each other.

Of course, we all have a dream job in mind, or a fantasy job that has little to do with reality. At my age, people want to work as little as possible for as much money as possible. Boys dream of becoming game testers, for example. Girls are different: they want to do something worthwhile that involves helping people. Really, I hate making sweeping statements, but I know far more girls than boys who want to become doctors. I'm sure there are girls who dream of becoming models or actresses, but they keep quiet about it, in view of the fact that boys are not known for their sensitivity when it comes to other people's dreams.

Most of us don't even really have a favourite subject at school and so we have no idea what job we might enjoy doing. Or people think they have to be realistic/pessimistic about their future career, because that shows how 'grown-up' they are. They come out with statements like 'No one here can ever make it as a world-famous actor, anyway.' I'd like to be a comic illustrator — or a postman, getting up just as day is dawning to deliver a few letters, then kicking back for the rest of the day. Or being the coolest teacher of all time.

Yes, sometimes I do think I just want to be a teacher, so I can make school less boring for kids. I mean, it's not even that hard to make yourself popular with students: don't set too much homework and know a little bit about TV series, films, and video games — that's all it takes. Then you'd be a god among teachers. But, on the other hand, there will always be those apathetic students who wouldn't even applaud the epic guitar solo I would play for them. I'd have to come up with something extra special for them.

8

The Blue Skeletons of November

or, what we're listening to when
we're wearing our headphones

I can't remember exactly when it began, but it was probably about a year ago that I started hearing loud beats and muffled voices emanating from my younger brother's room. At the dinner table, he would go on and on about the latest cool stuff his great idols had done: 'Jay Rock said this, but then The Game did that … and then 40 Glocc went … and then he dissed him and now he's on his shit list, and did you know Lil Wayne spent a year in Rikers?'

And so it goes on, the entire time. Somehow they've become his (anti)heroes. They're shallow, violent, tough, rich, and don't let anyone tell them what to do. They rap about beating their girlfriends, extorting protection money, celebrating their release from prison in strip clubs or at gangbangs, and about how their mothers gave up everything for them and they're gonna buy her a big house to live in one day.

I have no idea why my brother thinks all this is so cool. My bet is that he's impressed, or at least intrigued, by that exotic, taboo world. Fast cars, drugs, money, fame, fans — these are the things you think are good at his age. And rappers are cool, they have style, with their expensive gear and big gold chains. And there's nothing any of us want more than to be cool and accepted — by as many people as possible, preferably.

© Oskar Bühre

Rappers also represent the complete opposite to the morals and opinions of parents. That makes rappers the perfect vehicle for rebellion. And, just as it should be, my parents hate hip-hop. Of course, my brother is not the only one at our school who likes it. Practically every child between the ages of ten and fourteen listens to hip-hop. Sometimes in the playground at school, some Year Fives will rush up to us, spit some lines they've learned by heart, shout 'Hah, dissed you!' and then run away really quickly.

My brother now keeps on blaring out some lyrics or other that he's memorised, even though he has no idea what they mean. Recently, my parents had to explain to him why one lyric was homophobic. Once he'd understood, he realised they were right, saying he's never been keen on that particular artist anyway, and nobody really cares about what the lyrics say. Hardly an evening goes by when he's not showing my father another new video from some rapper or other. He thinks it's totally unfair that nobody else in our house has any time for this kind of music. 'Nobody likes my music!' And he's forced to listen to 'our' music.

Although I don't share my brother's love of hip-hop, his preference isn't always an ordeal for me. The truth is, I only watched the film *8 Mile* because of him — and ended up discovering not only a new favourite movie, but also a rapper whose music I really like: Eminem. His life story is told in the film, and he won an Oscar for the title song, 'Lose Yourself'. There's no denying Eminem has said and done a few stupid things in the course of his life — he was addicted to drugs and God knows what else — but somehow, I like him. Maybe it's because of that film, or because of my favourite song by him, 'Mockingbird'. It's a lullaby for his children in which he apologises for everything that's happened since he got famous.

In general, I listen to music because I like it and not because I want to be part of a particular group or because I want to annoy certain people. I've even taken over a few bands and artists from my parents, like The Beatles, Green Day, The Roots, Deftones, Slipknot, Cat Stevens, Simon & Garfunkel, Tom Waits, Neil Young, and Johnny Cash. I've been listening to most of these since I was a little child — The Beatles on long car journeys or Tom Waits at Christmas, for instance. If I do listen to hip-hop, it's just for fun, or because my brother insists on playing someone-or-other's latest track.

Hip-hop in general is still probably the most popular music, though. By contrast, there are very few heavy-metal or rock fans among us. I don't know what the problem is, but everyone pulls a face as soon as they hear guitar riffs and drums (except for a rare few who have discovered AC/DC).

Overall, at our age, we take a much more differentiated view of music. The charts are suddenly 'mainstream' and mainstream is shit and it's cool to like music that nobody else in the class has ever heard of. (Which makes it difficult for me, because I've always thought people should not just follow the charts when it comes to defining their music tastes. Now that everyone thinks this, too, I don't like it, and have started listening to *old* chart stuff, like Usher's 'Yeah!' or 50 Cent's 'Candy Shop'.)

My father is always telling me how people used to hone their personal taste in music by going into a record shop and browsing, to see what new releases had come out in their favourite genre. Nowadays, we look on Spotify to see what certain other people are listening to — such as the cool guy in Year Eleven, or somebody else everyone says knows what they're talking about. It's entirely possible that we'll end up listening to the same stuff as our parents or even our grandparents. Michael Jackson, for example, or Louis Armstrong.

In my class, at least, Spotify and YouTube have made music tastes so individual that I don't even recognise a lot of what my peers are listening to. Grouping together in tribes according to the music we listen to — like you see in films about punks, or mods and rockers — is unthinkable for us. Everyone listens to different stuff, and even hip-hop is no longer really a subculture. Guess what music my father put on recently when he was giving me a lift in his car? Exactly! It's the type of music that everyone can live with and it's seen as the coolest. And that's the point: you want to be seen to be listening to music that everyone likes. I would never put Simon & Garfunkel on when all my friends were round, for example.

So that's more or less what's going on under those headphones that not only Cristiano Ronaldo and David Beckham wear all the time, but every boy between the ages of twelve and sixteen. Often, we're not actually listening to anything, yet still keep the phones on, because we think it looks cool. It's also an excellent way to avoid getting into conversations, or just to take a five-minute break from everyone without having to go into long explanations about why.

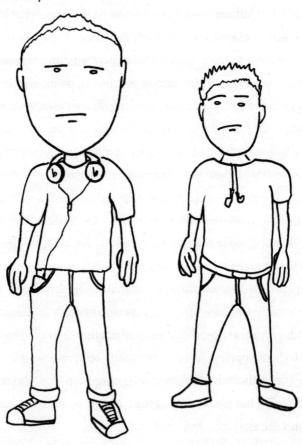

At the moment, headphones are almost more important than the music that comes out of them. They're a kind of status symbol. There are the big, fat expensive ones with plump ear cushions and the best sound — 'Beats by Dr Dre' are definitely greater than Sony as far as style, sound, and, unfortunately, price are concerned. And then there are the little white ones, mostly from Apple. Girls like to walk round the playground in pairs sharing them — one girl with a bud in her right ear, the other with a bud in her left ear — skipping along to the beat, or at least walking in lockstep to the rhythm.

Ah yes, dancing: girls find it easier than boys, or maybe they just get drunk quicker at parties. Anyway, nearly all the girls at a party will start dancing straightaway, whereas on our side it takes many litres of vodka and beer, as well as repeated encouragement from the girls, before a foot might even start tapping along with the beat — or against it. But in the end, everyone is hopping about, doing their impressions of John Travolta or Michael Jackson, or showing off that breakdance move they've practised for hours at home. Or unintentionally doing an impression of an epileptic having a fit. Sometimes, a circle will form and you get forced into the middle to show off your 'moves', although in our case those 'moves' are pretty lame — after all, we're not growing up in Los Angeles. You're more likely to spend your youth practising the tuba than breakdancing with your homies. Not that I have anything against the tuba, but you know what I mean.

Speaking of the tuba: most of us have played an instrument since primary school. By the age of thirteen at the latest, kids who only months ago were obediently practising *Peter and the Wolf* refuse to carry on, or at least insist on playing the music from *Titanic* instead. Or they ask for a set of drums for Christmas. Personally, I was lucky in the instrument I chose — I've been learning the guitar since forever.

Recently, I thought it might be cool to make some music with other people — not to enter a TV talent show, but just for a bit of fun, and because it's cool to have a band, and because, they say, it goes down well with the girls. So I asked my mates if they fancied starting a band, and they were all totally down with it. We planned to set up a proper rehearsal room in the garage at my house and buy some mikes, and then off we'd go! We already had a name before a single note had been played: The Blue Skeletons of November.

With a name like that, what could go wrong? When we met for our first practice session, we realised we didn't even know what kind of music we wanted to make. While Leo and I were trying to think what music we might make with two guitars and my brother's drum set, a dispirited Francis started rummaging through the junk in the garage. Eventually, he discovered a ski helmet and a pair of old boxing gloves, which he immediately put on.

We decided we would just jam. Francis had never played drums before in his life, but he didn't let that put him off. He whacked the cymbal so hard he broke the drumstick in half. He was pretty perturbed, but we assured him it happens even to the best of drummers. So he carried on with just one stick, using his right boxing glove like a real drummer while Leo and I tried to make him play more quietly because he was drowning out our acoustic guitars. But he couldn't hear us through the ski helmet. Leo and I were finally so frustrated that we just stormed out of the garage and went to my room to read comics. At some point, Francis joined us and started poking us with his one remaining drumstick.

I was in a pretty bad mood that afternoon. In my mind, I'd imagined we would be much more professional. Yes, you can't always get what you want ... and sometimes you really can't get no satisfaction!

That experience in the garage cured me of the idea of starting a band, but didn't put me off music for good. It can be vital for survival, especially while doing homework. My parents don't seem to agree with that, however. They claim it lowers my powers of concentration. On the contrary, I think music motivates you, because it makes studying less boring. There are people who can't concentrate properly while music is on, but I like to have it playing in the background — while I'm drawing, too. I find it does me good. Except when I'm doing something where I have to concentrate really hard, like physics or algebra. Then even I find music in the background a bit off-putting.

Apart from that, I sometimes need loud music to drown out the gangsta rap played by a certain person I live with. That said, my brother's taste is improving — at least he's listening to less music by local rappers, who are the ones I hate the most because there's always an ignorant, antisocial undertone to them. American rappers are probably the same, but we don't really listen as closely to what they're saying. Now my brother has turned fourteen and the situation seems to be returning to some semblance of normality. He's probably getting sick of listening to the same music all the time just so he can look like a rebel.

9

Conflict with Parents

or, why you should never call your
kids any stupid nicknames

Everything was so much simpler in the past! Yes, you're not the only one who thinks this — I do, too. In the past, I used to listen to the same music as my parents, and pretended to not like computer games and to think TV was boring. Books were the most exciting things in the world, because that's what my parents thought and I shared their opinion on that as I did on everything else. I even thought my parents were … can I even bring myself to use this adjective? … coo … No, I can't have thought that, surely? Anyway, the point is, we used to be something like mates.

I did everything I could to try to please my parents, and I wanted to grow up to be just like them. Everything my parents said was right, and everything that they thought was wrong was automatically bad. If I wanted to know something, I just asked my parents; they knew what was what. I avoided any problems with my parents, didn't argue, and questioned almost nothing that they said. You trust your parents implicitly, after all. Why complicate matters by thinking for yourself?

Yes, why do that? Well, because I can! That's why! I have to form my own opinions; I can't just take over my parents' way of seeing things. I want to be my own man, an independent human being, not a yes-man or somebody's puppet! That's what arguments in adolescence are there for, and that's why they're so important to us teenagers. It's strange that parents have such a hard time understanding this. The little boy who loved going out for walks or bike rides with Mum and Dad suddenly thinks nothing could be more crap and boring. The boy whose favourite subject was always art gets into an argument with his art teacher over a drawing project, resulting in the first — but certainly not last! — ever 'D' on his report card. It doesn't appear to bother him particularly, but his parents think he's stopped trying at school, got lazy. But, most importantly, they think he's deliberately picking fights with his teachers and that he's making his life harder than it needs to be.

Having said all that, I must also add that, in the grand scheme of things, I get on okay with my parents. Pretty cool, right? I just like to keep stress down to a minimum, so I do my homework, do alright at school, hang out with friends, read books, and don't spend as much time gaming as some people do … Low-maintenance is the adjective I'd use to describe someone like me.

And I'd describe my parents as basically laid-back. If I get a 'D' in maths, they'll offer help. (That's *offer*, not *force* — I can still talk my way out of it.) And when *Game of Thrones* is on, they make an attempt to stop me seeing the worst of the

126

beheading scenes or the most interesting of the bedchamber scenes, though I usually win the argument just by saying, 'And what about *Lord of the Rings*?' Of course, there isn't really any comparison between the two. 'People' are occasionally beheaded in *Lord of the Rings*, but it's rare, and when it does happen, the ones losing their heads are usually the filthy, evil Orcs, who deserve it anyway, and not all your favourite characters, like in Season Three of *Game of Thrones*.

Yes, I watch TV series with my mum and dad. In fact, they were the ones who got me addicted. It's my parents who I have to thank for my up-to-date knowledge on the subject of TV shows.

Although I actually get on quite well with my parents, my peace is sometimes shattered by differences of opinion between us. So, let's start with the innocuous problems, and move onto the more serious ones later. I might have brought some of them upon myself, but in other cases I am definitely an innocent victim. Anyway, you can judge for yourself:

I don't want to be treated like a baby anymore.

For example, I might be sitting on the couch, or anywhere else, minding my own business, and along comes my mother. She stares at my forehead with a surprised, almost shocked, look on her face.

Me (distraught and annoyed): 'Mum, please! Stop it!'

Mum (as if butter wouldn't melt in her mouth, while examining the growths on my forehead with fascination): 'What?'

Me: 'Please stop staring at my spots!'

Mum: 'But they don't look good at all. Let me at them, just a little. Or I'll get you an appointment with the beautician.'

Me (squeezing at my zits myself before she does): 'Oh, come on, leave me alone, can't you?!? Stop it, please!'

Mum: 'Alright, be like that, then.' (Dramatic sigh.)

For some reason, she gets a total kick out of squeezing my spots. Just to get this absolutely clear: I only let her do it to keep her quiet, otherwise she puts on her sad face and starts saying she wishes she had a daughter whose hair she could plait. What can I say? She's the only female in our family.

I don't want to be treated like a five-year-old, either!

When you're watching a film or video on the internet, you usually get pop-up ads of the most annoying kind. Various grannies or housewives are only one kilometre away and want to meet up with you … and only you, of course. Usually, the amount of clothing they're wearing ranges from not much to nothing at all. Whenever my mother catches a glimpse of them — SLAP! — she claps her hands over my eyes, and won't let me carry on watching my film until the ad has disappeared. Really.

Remind me, how old am I again? Three? Four? Ah, I'm five already! The same thing happens when we're watching a film and two characters start doing what people do when they love each other very, very much. With most things, my mother is normally quite laid-back, but when it comes to things like that:

Urgghh, no! Such representations of sex are bound to destroy my image of nature's most beautiful gift. As if it wasn't destroyed already.

And must you always act as if you're already ninety years old, and we're visiting you in the old people's home?

For example, when we're watching a film together: at the most exciting, or most tragic, or any other point in the movie — by two thirds of the way through the movie at the very latest — my parents always fall asleep, guaranteed. The next day, they can't remember a thing about the film and make you retell them the entire story from start to finish.

Parents: 'Who was the one with the eyes again?'

Me: 'Eh? Who?'

Dad: 'The one with the black hair!'

Me: 'Hrmmph, can you be more specific? The one with the nose or the one with the eyes? I've got no idea who you mean.'

Mum: 'There's no need to get snarky just because I can't remember. You know exactly who I mean.'

Me: 'Do you realise how many people in that film had black hair?'

I don't even know if they're being serious. Yesterday, after *Game of Thrones*, Mum asked me in all seriousness what 'the girl with the dragons' was called. Well, at least it's so bad it's funny …

You can be so embarrassing!

For example, why do you insist on calling me 'Paulie' in front
of my friends? I mean, what's that all about? My name is
Paul. Paul is fifteen and has hairs on his legs; Paulie is maybe
four years old and loves sweets. And when my friends come
round, you insist on giving them a hug and involve them
in a conversation that lasts for what feels like three hours.
Seriously? Save that for your own friends.

There's only one thing more embarrassing than that:
when you pick the time that my friends are round to suddenly
remember that I haven't tidied my room or emptied the
dishwasher yet. Can't I do it another time? If my friends
are round, we don't want to spend our time unloading the
dishwasher together. Just as I don't wait until your friends

are there to remind you that a certain someone has not done the washing and I have nothing to wear tomorrow.

You're far too nosey!

If I come home from school annoyed, worn out, or maybe even upset, I can guarantee that my mother will not stop nagging until she extracts the truth from me. For instance:

Paul arrives home. He missed the all-important penalty that would have won his team the match. He throws himself onto his bed and just wants to forget the whole episode.

Mum: 'Hello? Hey, why didn't you say hello when you came home?'

Paul grimaces: 'Hi, Mum.'

Mum: 'Paul, did something happen at school today?'

Paul: 'No!'

Mum: 'Is it girl trouble?'

Paul: 'Man, Mum, no it isn't. Now just leave me alone!'

Mum: 'Well, there's definitely something wrong.'

Paul (through gritted teeth): 'No, there isn't. Now go away.'

Mum: 'Did you fail a test?'

Paul: 'No, I didn't. I missed a penalty. Satisfied?'

Mum: 'Oh. Was it important?'

Paul: 'OH NO, MOTHER!!!!!! IT WAS ONLY THE SEMI-FINAL!!! Of course it was important. We could have been in the final!'

Mum (offended): 'I only asked.'

You're so unfair!

I've just settled down nicely on the couch for a well-earned read of my book. Well, it depends what you mean by well-earned; I haven't done my maths homework yet, but everybody needs a break. Just to relax — I don't have enough opportunity to do that as it is.

As if she could read my mind, my mother shouts from upstairs, 'Paul, you're not doing anything at the moment, could you go fetch some milk from the supermarket?'

Why is it always me? I can literally feel my brother laughing his head off in his room because he's managed to shirk a chore — again! Ever since he showed our mother an algebra equation-solving app on his phone, he's been legally able to do what he does anyway: nothing. He could show my mother a Google Maps screen and she'd believe him if he said he was using it to study.

This is when I remember why I never lie on the living-room couch to relax. Because no rest is permitted in this house. They'll always find something for me to do, unless I'm pretending to study, which is an automatic get-out-of-chores free ticket. And I'm now inwardly berating myself for my stupidity. But it's so typical — parents have no idea about the fair distribution of labour.

Instead of sharing out chores so everyone does the same amount of work, they take advantage of the one who is good natured and helpful (me). They can't be bothered dealing with one of my brother's scenes, so they'd simply rather ask the son they're less scared of. I mean, my brother hardly ever does anything, and when he does, he always gets a huge round of applause for it. I do three times as much as him every day, and what do I get? Even more chores. Some people might like that, but I think it's just unfair.

Maybe it has something to do with the fact that both my parents were younger siblings of older brothers who bullied them. Perhaps that's why they're so sensitive to the wishes of my little brother. Anyone who has brothers or sisters knows what I'm talking about. There's always one sibling who gets preferential treatment.

Everything always has to happen 'right now!'
Sometimes my parents forget that I'm slowly starting to live my own life.

Mum: 'Paul, can you come down and get your clean washing?'

Paul: 'Yes, in a minute!'

(Five minutes later.) Mum: 'Paul, I told you to come and get your clothes. They're still here. Come and get them right now!'

Paul: 'There's no need to fly off the handle, as usual. I'll be down in a minute.'

Mum: 'Not in a minute — now!'

Paul: 'No, I'm not coming.'

Mum: 'Don't make me come up there, young man!'

Paul: 'I haven't done anything!'

Mum (desperate): 'Will you please come and get your washing?'

Paul: 'In a minute.'

Mum explodes.

Paul: 'Mum, are you alright?'

You never let us do anything.

I'm actually lucky, compared to some of my friends. Some of their parents still check to make sure they only watch films that are classified for their age group. Which is totally stupid, because all it does is isolate their children from their friends who are already allowed to watch violent or explicit or adult-themed films. And if you don't let us watch TV series, it's as if someone stopped you from reading the newspaper, and you can't join in the conversation at the office water cooler.

Let's imagine everyone in your class is allowed to watch *True Blood* except you, because your parents won't allow it.

Tom: 'Hey, Jonas, did you see the last episode, when …'

Jonas: 'Stop, shut up, I haven't seen it yet!!! No spoilers, please!! Just keep your mouth shut!'

Tom: 'Okay, okay. What episode are you up to, then?'

Jonas: 'First episode of Season Three, when Sookie comes back from the world of the faeries …'

You: 'What's *True Blood* about, actually?'

Jonas: 'It's a vampire series. It's really bloodthirsty. So cool!'

Tom: 'Yeah, man, you've really got to watch it!'

You: 'I would if I could, but my parents won't let me.

There's a child-lock on my computer and I don't know how to turn it off.'

Tom: 'I had that, in Year Two.'

You leave, feeling like a total idiot.

And, most importantly: accept us the way we are!

Let me tell you about a friend of mine. Her father is a violist — or whatever a person who plays the viola is called — and her mother is a pianist and piano teacher. So, of course, she's expected to play an instrument, preferably two, and most preferably of all, the viola and the piano, of course. I mean, sure, both of them must have experienced great concerts and stuff, and they want their daughter to have the same opportunities.

Naturally, my friend puts a lot of effort into her music, because she wants to please her parents. But, somehow, it's never enough for her father. I think she plays brilliantly, but then I'm no expert. Her father is always finding fault with her playing — not clean enough here, not quite the right pitch there. She really does try her very best to please him, but in the end, it's always a disappointment. She's starting to blame herself, and keeps saying how untalented she is. But she's not only a gifted musician; she can paint really well, too. Oh, and she's a maths genius.

Whenever I ask her, she says it's her dream to play at the Philharmonie in Berlin or give a concert in New York, but I don't think that's really her dream at all. And then she has all the stress at school that comes from the fact that her parents have such high expectations. I'm always telling her she should allow herself some time off, but she says she enjoys school work and practising and won't listen to any arguments to the contrary. I thought she would begin to see things more clearly when she hit puberty, but it hasn't happened yet. We hardly ever see each other anyway, because she's always so busy.

The last time we did see each other, we went to a party and she got totally drunk. She burst into tears and told me she was due to go to America next year for an exchange year at a music school, and that she felt she couldn't cope with all the pressure anymore. She said she didn't want to go to a stupid music school, because everyone there would be better than her, and her parents don't care about her anyway, because they were busy arguing and constantly in a bad mood. I just did my best to console her, but I don't really know how to deal with people when they're drunk. I don't really think I helped her. Maybe just for that moment, at least. And she isn't the only child I know who feels they can't live up to their parents' expectations. Not by far.

Actually, when I think about it, it seems to me that all major conflicts between parents and their children boil down to the fact that the parents are disappointed in their offspring, to a lesser or greater degree, because they haven't turned out the way the parents would have wished. I think parents often don't realise this until puberty kicks in and their children are already almost grown up, and are likely to change only minimally, if at all. And I think children just don't react well to that feeling. They start to be unhappy with themselves, although they can't change the way they are.

I think my parents have sometimes wondered why their second son was listening to gangsta rap. And I think they'd prefer it if I didn't read so many fantasy books and comics, but they've accepted it now. So the best thing is to try to accept your children the way they are, otherwise your demands might break them.

It goes without saying that it's not always easy to do that — which brings us conveniently to the topic of the next chapter: parenting.

10

Parenting

or, what you need to know according
to a person directly affected by the issue

Sometimes, parents are so overwhelmed by the challenges of their children's adolescence that they seek professional help. From a book. A parenting-advice book, to be precise. There is nothing wrong with that. But once that book falls into the hands of their children, it's all over.

That's what happened in my case. It was a beautiful sunny day, and I was in a fine mood, having finished my school and homework duties, and I was about to reward myself with a few episodes of an exciting TV series. The only problem was that the laptop battery was flat, so off I went in search of the power cable. But no matter where I looked, I just couldn't find it, and I began to suspect that my mother had hidden it as a way of reducing my screen time. Very clever, mother!

There was one place I still hadn't looked, however, a chamber I rarely enter: my parents' bedroom. I climbed the narrow staircase step by step until I reached the third floor of our small townhouse. I opened the door, and then I saw it. Not the computer cable; oh, if only it had been the computer cable! It was lying on my parents' bedside table and at first it barely even caught my attention. But when I spotted the word *Puberty*, I became intrigued. It was the title of a book. Beneath that word, a smaller, but still bold-type text read: *when your kids know it all and you can't teach them a thing*. And then in even smaller letters: *plain sailing in stormy seas*. It was written by a certain Jesper Juul. And the cover was emblazoned with a picture — half in shadow, like the personification of all evil — of a pair of totally ugly Converse, the kind teenagers like to wear.

An uneasy feeling crept over me: Why did my parents need to read this book? Were they so unable to cope with my brother and me? Somehow, I felt betrayed. I mean, are you kidding? If you have a problem with me, talk to me about it — don't look for answers in a book! When they bought it, my parents were probably hoping it would tell them how to regain control over me, or how to survive this change without sustaining permanent damage.

Oh no, dearest parents, you won't get away with this so easily. True to the motto 'know thine enemy', I decided to soak up every single page of this book like a sponge, to rob them of their ultimate weapon. I read it from cover to cover. One thing I noticed right away was that Juul admits he's not a parenting expert, and says such a thing doesn't even exist. Pretty puzzling, I thought. The blurb on the back of the book hails him as 'the shining light of modern educational theory' and as 'one of our most important and innovative family therapists'. Aha, I thought to myself, the old 'I'm not the messiah! He is the messiah!' number from *The Life of Brian*. Well, I'm not falling for that one. Oh no!

Anyway, the author turned out not to be particularly interested in providing answers, apparently considering it more important to ask questions. Yeah, take your time, J.J., you've got nearly two hundred pages to fill, after all! The next chapter heading really made me start to wonder: 'Puberty is a fact, not a sickness'. Can't argue with that, I suppose. But then I read, 'Their brains are reorganising.' That's why we're unable to consider the consequences of our actions. WTF?! Seriously, Juul believes that the part of the brain responsible for the anticipation of consequences is incapacitated in eighty-five per cent of teenagers. That's a biological fact, allegedly, so I shouldn't take it personally. Can I please be part of the fifteen per cent and not the eighty-five? Please?

I mean, I know what the consequences of my actions are. An example: If I hit my brother, he will either hit me back or run away. He's also likely to start bawling like a baby and, since he's such an incredibly talented actor, I will definitely get into trouble with my parents. But I know in advance it will be worth it. I think that can be called forward-looking action. So there is nothing broken in my brain. I hope not, at least.

To be honest, there are a couple of people in my class who've always made me wonder what they must be thinking of when they're screaming and shouting in lessons while hurling balls, chalk, books, sponges, or any other potential projectile across the classroom. Are they, like me, aware of the consequences of their actions, but simply couldn't give a shit? I believe we teenagers are perfectly capable of thinking about the consequences of our actions. Might it be that the idea of something being biologically wrong with us is nothing more than a crutch for adults, to help them put up with us more easily? The simple truth is that we are almost never bothered about rules, limits, or unpleasant consequences.

So maybe something is broken, after all. It's hard for me to judge because I'm directly affected. But it does give us an excellent excuse. The next time I get into trouble, I can just blame my broken brain. Thanks, J.J.!

In battles with my parents, I can, of course, make excellent tactical use of this knowledge. I intend to try it out the next time an opportunity presents itself:

Paul: 'Mum, I don't feel well.'

Mum: 'What's wrong?'

Paul: 'Dunno.'

Mum: 'Where does it hurt?'

Paul: 'My head feels funny.'

Mum: 'Ah, you have a headache. Why didn't you say so? I'll get you a painkiller.'

Paul: 'No, a tablet won't help. It feels like someone's building something inside my head. No, building's not the right word. More like someone's making alterations. D'you know what I mean?'

Mum: 'Paul, what are you talking about? You haven't been … ?' (She leans forward and looks into my eyes suspiciously.) 'No, your pupils look perfectly normal. Maybe we really should take you to the doctor.'

Paul: 'It feels like only half my brain is working. I think that's why I'm so bad at maths now.'

Mum: 'Rubbish! What are you talking about?'

Paul: 'Do you think puberty can make you sick?'

Mum: 'No, I don't. Now, will you finally tell me what's wrong with you?'

Paul: 'Do you still like me, Mum, even though I'm going through puberty now?'

Mum: 'Of course I do, why are you asking such a question?'

Paul: 'Am I difficult?'

Mum: 'Well, sometimes.'

Paul: 'I'm sorry.'

Mum: 'No need to apologise; it's not that bad.'

Paul: 'I'm just not very good at thinking about the consequences of my actions.'

Mum: 'Who's been telling you rubbish like that?'

Paul: 'No one. I read it.'

Mum: 'And where, might I ask?'

Paul: 'In that puberty book you've got upstairs in your room. Am I so bad that you need a book to tell you how to cope? Am I really so hard to understand?'

Mum: 'Oh, Paul, I'm sorry! I just wanted to see what he has to say. There are one or two good tips in it!'

Paul: 'You don't like me anymore!'

Mum: 'Paul, don't say that. You know I like you.'

Paul: 'Why did you buy that book, then?'

Mum: 'I don't know. I'm sorry.'

Perfect! She's putty in my hands. Now I can get anything I want:

Paul: 'It's okay. Will you buy me a new stereo system?'

Mum: 'No, why?'

Paul: 'Well, mine's broken and I thought ...'

Mum: 'You can buy a new one yourself.'

Oh, well, almost anything.

Only joking — but it is annoying when everyone acts as if we were the most problematic group of human beings in the world, with the possible exception of Islamic extremists. When you enter a newsagency, you're guaranteed to see at least one picture of a truculent-looking boy or a rebellious-looking girl staring out at you from the cover of a special-edition magazine about adolescence. Our children — who are they really?

Our brains are not just being reorganised, they're possibly being damaged by all the porn we consume from an early age, or the constant gaming we're addicted to. Apparently, we don't know what tenderness is and don't face any real challenges anymore. And boys cope less well than girls with everything, allegedly. It all makes it sound like we're an inferior, primitive race of subhumans. I sometimes wonder how all those complaining, criticising pensioners manage to forget that they were once exactly like us. Surely we can't be so abnormal?

Despite his advanced age, Juul has not forgotten. He

sees teenagers as human beings, which is one thing I like about his book. Seriously, there are one or two things I think we can learn from J.J.

That you shouldn't control and monitor your children's every move. That parents should let children make their own experiences in life. That you should accept the fact that all sorts of things go wrong in families, and children aren't perfect.

It's like everything in life — there is never one single solution to all problems. All in all, it seems as if Juul is in fact precisely what he claims not to be: a parenting expert. Okay, he is a little outdated: for example, he has no advice on computer games. But, all in all, he's a pretty okay guy.

But there were so many questions that kept springing to mind while I was reading his book: Why are adults so at sea when it comes to adolescence? Why do they have such trouble understanding us? I mean, like I said, they've been through puberty, too, after all. Why is it so difficult for them to think back to what it was like and put themselves in our position? Maybe they really have forgotten how it was. But why, then, do they turn for advice to someone with exactly the same memory problem as them rather than asking us kids? Okay, maybe it's because we're uncommunicative and moody, especially when they try to talk to us about this stuff.

To pre-empt all misunderstandings, I present here Ten Commandments for my parents to follow when interacting with me, if they want to survive my adolescence unscathed:

1.   Thou shalt leave me in peace.

2.   Thou shalt not enter my room, except when
   • you are bringing clean sheets or breakfast in bed
   • there is an emergency and someone is in real danger
   • I have overslept and you're waking me up for school
   • there is cake
   • you are requesting an audience with me.

3. Thou shalt not give me orders. I will not accept them, but will answer, if at all, only to requests or well-intentioned advice.

4. However, it remains up to me to decide whether to follow or ignore such advice, since, after all, I am the one who must live with the consequences. This also means that I will only tidy my room when I feel like it, and not whenever you want.

5. Thou shalt cook me food when I'm hungry.

6. Thou shalt accept bad grades swiftly, without constant questions and recriminations. I normally know why they were bad, and if I don't I will ask for help.

7. Thou shalt not try to force me to do things I don't feel like doing. If you do, I won't talk to you again.

8. Thou shalt support me in everything I do. I still need your help, even though I can't admit it to your face. I am trying to become independent, and if I ask you openly for help, the illusion will be shattered.

9. Thou shalt try not to worry so much about me.

10. Thou shalt realise that I'm not being like this just for

fun, or to hurt you, but because it's the only way I can grow up. So don't take offence.

11. Thou shalt know: whatever happens, and whatever it may look like — I still love you.

11

Mood Swings

or, what to take seriously
(while not freaking out)

You often feel pretty shit when you're going through puberty. You're stressed, unhappily in love, and spotty. Everyone knows about these adolescent states of mind, and that's why you often hear these words: 'I'm not feeling too good right now.' Before I come to the real, serious issues, let me put your mind at ease: those words do not always mean that we're actually not feeling well. Most often, it's just an excuse for failing a test, or so that we can stay at home and relax on a Sunday when our parents want to drag us out to the museum before we finally grow out of such family outings for good. As a parent, in situations like that, you simply have to consider whether you would prefer to put your child through a hideous ordeal, or leave him or her in peace.

But sometimes it is more than that. You might not have a headache or stomach-ache, but you still feel shit. You don't have girlfriend/boyfriend problems and your beloved pet hasn't just snuffed it, but you still feel sad. You should really be doing your homework or doing *something* at least, but instead you're lying on your bedroom floor, staring at the ceiling and asking yourself what the point of it all is. You want to scream, cry, do something, but you just lie there feeling sorry for yourself. You're depressed.

I think everyone has felt sad or frustrated at some time without really knowing why. I think it's more severe in some people than others. On a scale of one (feeling listless) to ten (feeling suicidal), I would place myself at about five. The problem is that most people think feeling depressed is the same as feeling suicidal, or that it means you're going to start cutting yourself or self-harming. But feelings of depression can be stronger or weaker, just like a cold can be heavy or light. Sometimes you have the sniffles, sometimes you have a nasty bout of the flu or an annoying sore throat that you can't shake off. Sometimes there's some stupid reason for depressive feelings, and sometimes they turn up when you're least expecting them. I once saw a film in which depression was described as like being under water, and I think that's a fitting comparison. It breaks over you like a huge wave and threatens to drown you.

With me, I suddenly get the feeling that everything is too much, and I can't see how I'm ever going to be able to cope with this thing called life. I've found the best strategy is to talk about it, or to watch either sad movies or feel-good movies, or to play sport to take my mind off things. Sometimes, the feeling goes away again quickly; other times, it just won't go away, whatever I do.

You definitely need someone to talk to, someone who will take the initiative, because sometimes you just can't shake it off without someone else's help, or without a friend or a family member to give you a good kick up the backside. That's how it is for me, at least. I'd rather have someone say directly to my face that they're sick of me just lying around on the couch all day brooding than ask cautiously if I wouldn't rather be doing something more productive. Although it is difficult for others to know how best to react.

Via Facebook I found out that a girl I was in preschool with is now seriously depressed and properly suicidal. Her cover photo on Facebook is a really bleak photo with a dead tree, crows, and a gravestone, with a comment saying something like, '*Someday I just won't wake up and my suffering will have an end.*'

I really didn't know how to react when I saw this. On the one hand, it does look like some kind of cry for help; on the other hand, it's difficult to know how serious someone really is. When it comes down to it, I didn't really know the person at all. Maybe she needed all the horrified comments on Facebook to show her that there are a lot of people out there who would miss her. Should I have just sent her a chat message saying, 'Hey, it looks like you're thinking of killing yourself. Is that right?' The last thing you want to do is say the wrong thing.

I'm really not going to presume to be able to explain what drives people to harm themselves or to consider suicide. We've certainly never learned about these things in biology lessons, or any other lessons, at school. It's probably just too important an issue to bother covering in lessons.

I think a lot of things have to come together, and you probably have to have a certain tendency already, for you to start thinking about ending your own life. I think people who reach that point must have extremely low self-esteem and have suffered at the hands of others. It must be pretty shitty if you don't have parents who love you. At our age, we don't have anyone except one or two friends, and our parents, who are supposed to think the world of us. And if you can't accept and love yourself the way you are, then I really wonder what keeps you from just 'ending it all'.

Luckily, I've never been that badly depressed. I'm just sometimes mega-frustrated, restless, and in a bad mood, and these feelings have got stronger since I started going through puberty. Not everyone has the courage to seek therapy, although that can be an excellent solution. A psychologist who has a different, more objective view and can give you an unbiased appraisal is useful in a situation like that. They might see things you would never have thought of, or notice things that you think are completely normal, but aren't.

Talk of therapy and psychologists might seem a bit extreme. You might be picturing an elderly gentleman in a white coat trying to treat a lunatic who can do nothing but stare catatonically into space. But a psychologist is nothing more than a pleasant listener who asks questions every now and then. Most people find just getting things off their chest is a great help.

People can convince themselves that their problem isn't so serious and they can cope with it alone, but this isn't the case with really bad depression. I'm talking from personal experience here. I have a lot of difficulty accepting other people's advice, but when I do, it usually turns out to be for the best. 'Don't knock it till you've tried it' is the phrase that springs to mind. It's most difficult the first time, but it gets a tiny bit easier to talk about each time. Though it remains a challenge, nonetheless.

Back when I was feeling bad, my parents realised pretty quickly what was going on with me, and I'm still grateful to them for that. They didn't waste any time. My mother had had similar feelings at my age. Usually, it's difficult to talk to your parents about something like that. You actually feel like you want to create some space between them and you, but it's helpful to have someone who knows exactly what you're going through because they've been through it, too. At times like that, it's really good to know that you're not alone with your problems.

Which doesn't mean that parents should constantly spy on their children or read their diaries. It means they should do their best to try to find out what state of mind their child is in. When it comes to cases like this, questions are more than welcome, even if the person in question denies it. I know — I've had days when I've said I didn't want to talk, but meant the complete opposite. Often, all it takes is a little shove in the right direction, and then everything comes bursting out.

So asking questions is good in this case, and it really does help to talk. If your parents don't understand you and you don't want to go straight to a psychologist, then there might be someone like a school counsellor, or a sports coach who understands where your head is at. Or a really good friend who you can tell everything to because you know he or she will never judge you for it. Everyone has to find out for themself what's best for them.

And you have to learn to live with your problems and your quirks in a way that allows you to like yourself and allows the people you like to like you, too. You should never despair or give up, but just keep picking yourself up and working on yourself. I don't believe it suddenly gets better after puberty, like flicking a switch, because every phase of life holds its own challenges. What's easy, for example, about finding the right job when you know you're going to be doing it every day for years to come?

But I do think it gets better the older and more experienced you get. At some point, you know who you are and what's best for you. So remember — it gets better.

12

Me and Others

or, what teens care about
besides themselves

Teachers tell us we have no passions, and our parents think we're boring. We're always being criticised for not caring about anything and for being too passive about everything. We're all consumerist zombies addicted to brand names and wi-fi, dragging ourselves through life and staying in bed till three p.m. on weekends. Without WhatsApp and Skype, we are nothing. Our only humour is based on Facebook videos, and we're incapable of concentrating on anything for longer than ten minutes. Meanwhile, because everything is so easy to find on the internet, we've lost the ability to wait or to 'earn' anything, so we're all impatient and spoilt. And what do we zombies really want? Our phones? A stable internet connection? A McDonald's close by?

Are there actually people who think that about us? Who don't see us as human beings, but as pests? If there are, then I'd like to make it quite clear right here and now: we are actual human beings. Just like every other human being in the world, we have dreams and desires, and, most importantly, plans for the future. And just because we all carry the same smartphones or wear similar clothes, we don't all share one big, communal brain. We are as diverse as any other group of people, even if we do invest so much energy in trying to disguise it.

Each human being is different, that should really go without saying. My personal ambition, for example, is to create my own comic series; my brother, on the other hand, might want to work with cars, and my friend Fred wants to play rugby professionally. Others haven't decided yet what their goals will be. We're just at the threshold of our adult lives, after all.

Some of us are ambitious, and do every bit of homework set so we can get a top-class degree from Harvard or Oxford. Others are afraid to do anything that involves leaving their hometown. Some even continue going to church after they've been confirmed. And for many of us who are ambitious, our parents are ambitious, too. They want us to get good grades at school, and to be good at football, or painting, or whatever it may be that interests us. They want us to do our best at all times. So most of us have at least one out-of-school activity to attend every weekday, whether it's daily tennis training plus tournaments at the weekend, or piano lessons three times a week plus football training twice. After all, if you want to be really good at something, you have to invest time and effort in it. For some, this might be okay, but for others, it can mean real stress.

In sports like football and hockey in particular, competitiveness starts early: first team or reserves, starting line-up or subs bench, along with pressure from parents desperate to have a superstar in the family. For some, that pressure is reason enough to give up. I found it quite a burden myself. I played a few tennis matches in tournaments, against opponents from other clubs. The most common type I faced was a little boy dressed up in tennis whites, with a bag that's twice as big as he is. On the bench at the side of the court, his father would be sitting, barking out orders to his son, telling him to concentrate for God's sake, or to work harder, or whatever. That was what really put me off. I mean, the poor lad was at least five years younger than me, and as thin as a rake — how was he supposed to return my balls?

Anyway, experiences like that are among the reasons why I'm not really keen on sporting competitions. I hate that grim, desperate determination to win. Even if you do win, you feel bad because you know the other boy's disgruntled father will be berating him in the car on the way home.

Another thing we care about is our friends and family — yes, this is even more important to us than the latest iPhone. When a friend in my class broke his collarbone, I visited him in hospital twice, with two different groups of people. My brother was in hospital for a week once, too, with a dodgy appendix. I was at his bedside almost every day, and brought him *Batman* comics to read. He never actually read them, though, because they had video on demand in his room, but still. When the chips are down, we are there for each other.

And the future is something we care about, too. After all, we're the ones who are going have to live in it. Although most people I know aren't actually willing to do much to preserve the planet. I always thought I had a 'social conscience', although I'd never been to a protest or done anything political. I didn't even get a 'Nuclear power? No thanks' sticker after Fukushima, like most people did. And I shop at H&M, whose clothes are probably manufactured in conditions that are not exactly the best for the workers. Although, if you asked me, I wouldn't be able to name a shop where I could buy my clothes instead.

Would I be prepared to go out and protest against something? To join a political party to make a change? No. To be perfectly honest, I just stick my head in the sand and refuse to waste my energy on something that I can't change anyway. There's nobody in my class who goes out to the demos on International Workers' Day to fight neo-Nazis, or who joins sit-down protests with refugees to raise awareness of their problems. Well, there are a few people on Facebook who post stuff about that kind of thing. But it's much easier to like a post or to follow the Greens on Twitter than to get your arse up off the couch, let alone actually leave the house.

In fact, we're all still pretty much under the influence of our parents when it comes to politics. Personally, my leanings are somewhere between the centre and the left. My parents vote Green — not because they're old hippies or do-gooders or anything, or because they're particularly interested in politics, or even because they know even one

Green politician by name. They vote Green out of principle, because, as they point out, the Greens were the first ones to bring the environment, energy policy, and all that to the public's attention. Nowadays, every party claims to be 'environmental'. Even the hard right have got the message. I don't really care who's in government, as long as they think at least a little bit more sustainably than before.

Our class teacher is always telling us we should be more appreciative of how lucky we are. He tells us there has never been such a long period of peace before. As far as 'appreciating how good we have it' is concerned, I actually think he's right. We have it so good that there's nothing we feel the need to go out and fight for.

In the past, by contrast, there was a lot for adolescents to fight for, and against. The baby boomers, for instance, who are always held up to us as a shining example of how politically active young people used to be. They really did have reason to protest. So much was broken and wrong, even I would probably have run out onto the street to shout out in anger.

But, today, what is there to shout about, and who is there to shout at? More money for everyone, fuck racism, fuck the NSA, fuck nuclear power! Nobody supports nuclear power anymore, nobody, except for a few mentally disturbed people. Nobody is racist or homophobic. Everyone listens to Macklemore's song 'Same Love', where he explains why he supports equal rights for homosexuals. And every class has children whose parents weren't born in this country.

Everything's just become normal.

Not long ago I read an article accusing students of being too conformist or docile. It said they were more interested in asking their teachers what the prescribed line spacing is for their essays, than questioning, let alone rebelling against, the bigger picture.

I think I know why that is. When you graduate from primary to high school, you're suddenly confronted with thousands of ludicrous official requirements: the maths teacher insists your arrows are long and narrow and by no means blocked in with ink, otherwise he will mark you down; in physics, the rule is completely the opposite. One teacher wants margins of at least four centimetres in width, the other wants half the page left blank, while yet another couldn't give shit about your margins, as long as you write something. And if you don't do it just the way they like it, you lose marks — it's counted as an actual mistake, 'poor presentation', and you're marked down an entire grade. So students spend most of their time trying to conform to some crazy requirements that have nothing to do with the content of the work. So it shouldn't be surprising that we don't go out and question the whole of society when we leave school.

Once, because I wanted to prove to myself that I'm not some indifferent consumerist zombie, and because I was interested to see what would happen, I joined a team of people standing for election to the student council at school. Our opponents were the young conservatives, and they took the whole thing deadly seriously. I had no idea beforehand that there really are people who care a lot about politics. Now I know. They made long speeches, shook each other's hands earnestly before the vote, et cetera. In fact, everything was smooth and well rehearsed, like on TV.

Anyway, the opposing team took the podium first and made a pretty impressive speech — about using your vote to make a change and not voting last year's 'clowns' (who weren't actually that bad) back in. They stared earnestly into the audience, spoke for a long time, and kept thumping the lectern to stop their listeners from falling asleep. At the end, they handed out gummy bears. Smart move. They also made lots of unrealistic promises, just like in the real elections.

We were more realistic, and that was our downfall. We just told people what we could deliver (a football tournament, school projects, a student-council trip) and what we couldn't (snack vending machines, allowing kids to spend free periods at home). There's only so much you can change in one year. Eventually, the young conservatives won, with twice as many votes as us.

And thus ended my first attempt to get political.

Acknowledgements

I was never alone while I was writing this book. There are so many friendly, helpful people who supported me, and this book wouldn't exist if it wasn't for them. I would like to thank them all. And then there are the people who appear in this book, unknowingly, or even against their will. To them, I would like to apologise.

I'll start with the apologies, just because I have a guilty conscience. First of all, I'd like to apologise to my mum and dad. I had to use you as examples of confused parents. I'm devastated that that meant I had to ignore some of your best qualities, while adding a few negative ones. You are the best parents in the entire world. But you know that already.

I also have to apologise to my dear brother. You might be the only person in the world who can constantly take the piss out of me and really, really annoy me, but you are brilliant, really! And lazy. But you are and always will be my brilliant brother.

Now to my school. Where should I start? Probably best to start with the girls. Girls, I'm sorry, I really am.

And to the boys: you can sometimes be really annoying, and sometimes I can be really annoying, too, but deep down inside, you're alright. Every one of you. You're good mates. So are the girls, by the way. And then there's our teachers. The chemistry teachers get a particularly bad rap. If I'm really honest, I kind of already liked chemistry a teeny bit, even before I saw *Breaking Bad*. But you know that already.

Now, some words of thanks. Let's start at the beginning. All this started with my work experience at *Zeitmagazin*, and from there, it just exploded. So I hereby blame the entire editorial staff for this book! A large vote of thanks goes, of course, to the boss, Christoph Amend — thanks, Christoph, for giving me this opportunity. Next comes the woman without whose help I would never have got that work-experience placement: thank you, Christine Meffert. And now to the great 'Master Mind' herself: Heike Faller. That was real teamwork. Thank you, Heike, for giving up your time for me.

Then comes Alexander Simon. Without you, I would never in my life have even dreamed of writing a book. Thanks, too, for the great time during the autumn holidays, when you gave me a place in the agency where I could sit and write without being disturbed, and where I had the opportunity to meet so many nice people. I would also like to thank my editor, Bettina Eltner, and my German publisher, Ullstein Verlag. Thank you, Bettina, for your constant support for my work and your constant supply of new ideas for the book. And, of course, a huge thank you goes to the entire staff at Ullstein.

Then there are the people who are not in the book business who I'd like to thank: an enigmatic knight, a woodcutter, and a dancer — all of them professional *LoL* players who gave me a glimpse of their mysterious world. And all the people I pestered with my questions about WhatsApp.

Finally, I'd like to thank everyone who was involved in any of the experiences I describe in this book.